CaseGrader: Microsoft® Office Excel® 2007 Casebook with Autograding Technology

FEATURES OF THIS PRODUCT INCLUDE:

- Hands-on, challenging Excel projects
- Realistic, case-based assignments that efficiently test your ability to combine multiple skills in Excel
- Instant grade results with feedback incorporated right into your Excel data file
- Step-by-step performance tracking that enables you to easily identify and target areas for improvement

//COURSE**PORT** SM

BELOW IS YOUR KEY CODE TO LOG IN TO COURSEPORT

To create a CoursePort account:

1. Launch your Web browser to http://login.course.com.
2. Click the New User Registration link.
3. Complete all required fields on this form, and then click Continue.
4. Confirm the Login Information and then click Continue.
5. On the Choose Your Product screen, scroll down until you find this title in the list, and then click the check box to the left of the title.
6. Enter the keycode found on this card.

XL07-89EF-7DF9-B9E2

Once you have registered, your Key Code cannot be reused.

7. Click the link to the product to launch CaseGrader.
8. To submit your completed files for grading, you will need to join a class by entering a Class Code. Click the Join A Class link and then enter the information.

WHAT IS COURSEPORT?

CoursePort provides a central location from which you can access Thomson Course Technology's online learning solutions with convenience and flexibility.

- Utilize a Universal Gradebook to track and share the work you complete with your instructor.
- Simplify your course work and the need to keep track of multiple passwords.
- Take advantage of CoursePort's tailored services including personalized home pages and simple tab navigation.

CaseGrader: Microsoft Office Excel 2007 Casebook with Autograding Technology

Thad Crews

Chip Murphy

THOMSON
COURSE TECHNOLOGY

Australia • Canada • Mexico • Singapore • Spain • United Kingdom • United States • Japan

CaseGrader: Microsoft Office Excel 2007 Casebook with Autograding Technology

is published by Thomson Course Technology.

Vice President of CTIS Strategic Business Unit:
Nicole Jones Pinard

Director of Product Technology:
Rachel Goldberg

Senior Editor:
Amanda Young Shelton

Technology Assistant:
Joel Tejada

Marketing Manager:
Kristin Taggart

Developmental Editors:
Robin Romer, Mary-Terese Cozzola

Contributing Author:
Kirk Atkinson

Manuscript Quality Assurance Testers:
Marianne Snow, Serge Palladino, Christian Kunciw

Production Editors:
Summer Hughes, Danielle Chouhan

Composition:
GEX Publishing Services

Text Designers:
Abby Scholz, GEX Publishing Services

Cover Designer:
Marissa Falco

GET INSTANT FEEDBACK ON YOUR MICROSOFT OFFICE EXCEL SKILLS WITH CASEGRADER!

CaseGrader: Microsoft Office Excel 2007 Casebook with Autograding Technology is designed to take your skills to the next level by offering you instant feedback on 12 case-based Microsoft Excel assignments. You'll get hands-on experience as you work live in the Excel application on challenging, real-life projects in this workbook. Once completed, simply upload your assignments to CaseGrader's secure Web portal to receive instant feedback.

CaseGrader allows you to:

❖ Get additional practice working with challenging Microsoft Excel 2007 assignments.

❖ Efficiently test your ability to combine multiple skills in Microsoft Excel 2007 through completing realistic case-based assignments.

❖ See grades instantly and view feedback incorporated right into your Excel data file.

❖ Track your performance in the secure gradebook to easily identify and target areas for improvement.

FROM THE AUTHOR

I love teaching! I love working one-on-one with students to help them learn new ideas and understand new concepts. Furthermore, teaching is in my blood. My father is a retired college professor, and my grandmother taught in a one-room school house in Missouri. In my opinion, there is no better job than being a teacher.

Even though I love teaching, I hate grading. I hate spending hours upon hours each week sitting at my desk trudging through homework submissions. Grading is obviously important, and the best grading is timely, detailed, and consistent. This is why we developed CaseGrader. It gives students the prompt, detailed feedback that benefits learning, and it grades the entire class with consistency and accuracy. It also gives me more time for the best part of teaching, interacting with my students.

If you are new to this product, thank you for giving us a try. I think you will be pleased with the result. If you are a returning user, welcome back. We rewrote all our cases for this edition, building on the best elements of our previous edition and making them better, while introducing the newest features of Excel 2007.

I hope you enjoy working with Excel 2007 and using CaseGrader 2007.

Thad Crews, Ph.D.
Associate Professor, CIS
Western Kentucky University

USING CASEGRADER—*FOR STUDENTS*

CaseGrader is straightforward and easy-to-use. Simply follow the directions below to set up your CaseGrader account and get started.

Getting Started

The first step to using CaseGrader is to set up your CaseGrader account through CoursePort. To set up your account, follow the directions found on the bound-in CoursePort card in the front inside cover of this workbook. After you have created your student account, you will have access to the CaseGrader application.

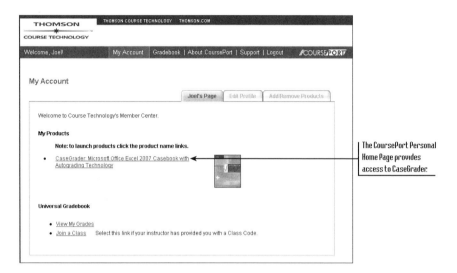

The CoursePort Personal Home Page provides access to CaseGrader.

Download Data Files

Each case has one or more data files, also called start files, that you will use as a starting point to complete the steps in the case.

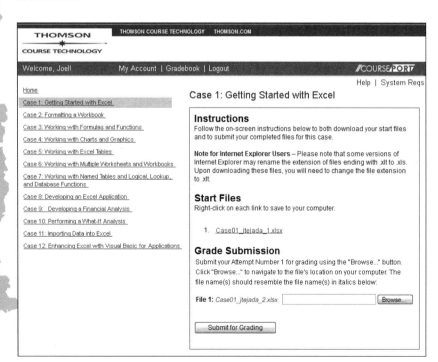

1. To access the data files for each case, open your Web browser and go to *http://casegrader2007. course.com*

2. Enter your username and password to access the CaseGrader Web site.

3. The CaseGrader home page will open. Using the left navigation menu, click the link for the case you are working on and follow the directions on the case page to download data files.

Submit Files for Grading

After you have completed all the steps in a case and have checked your work, it is time to submit the file for grading. (*Important Note:* You must be assigned to a class in order to submit files for grading. If your instructor has not already shared the Class Code with you, be sure to ask for it before you submit completed files.)

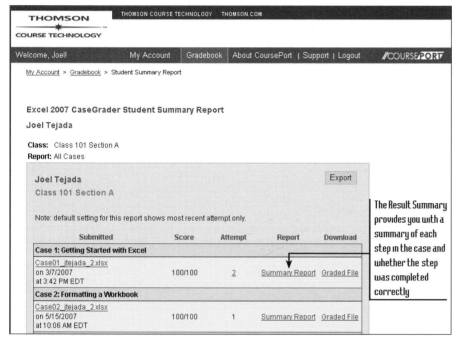

1. To submit files for grading, click the **Browse** button, located under the *Grade Submission* section on the case page, and navigate to the file location on your computer. Your file name should resemble the file name that appears before the Browse button in italics. Then, click the **Submit for Grading button**. CaseGrader will take a few moments to grade the file. All submissions for each case are recorded.

2. To view your results, click the **Gradebook** link at the top of the page.

3. To view the Result Summary report for each submission, click the **Summary Report** link in the Gradebook.

USING CASEGRADER—*FOR INSTRUCTORS*

The case projects in the CaseGrader casebook are designed to be easily incorporated into any full-semester course on Microsoft Excel 2007. The projects can easily be used with any Microsoft Excel textbook, including *New Perspectives on Microsoft Excel 2007*, *Shelly/Cashman's Microsoft Excel 2007-Comprehensive*, or *Illustrated Microsoft Excel 2007* just to name a few. There are mapping grids available at *www.course.com* for these other Microsoft Excel 2007 textbooks to make integrating the CaseGrader into your course a breeze.

Maximizing the Benefits of Using CaseGrader

To maximize the benefits of using CaseGrader in your course, it is important to understand all of the functionality features available. CaseGrader allows you to:

❖ Adjust the settings for each case, including setting the maximum number of submissions allowed, the maximum and minimum scores for an assignment, and the point values of each task in a given assignment.

❖ View detailed information on each student's performance, including the number of times a student has submitted a project and associated grades for each submission. You can also download a graded version of the student's file to pinpoint where that student may need additional help.

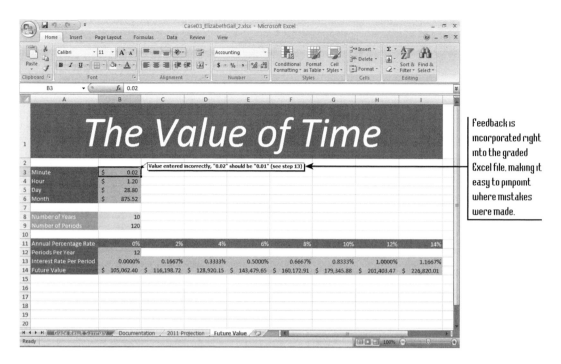

Feedback is incorporated right into the graded Excel file, making it easy to pinpoint where mistakes were made.

❖ View a Results Summary report for each graded data file. Using the Result Summary report, you can tell at-a-glance which tasks were completed correctly, or incorrectly.

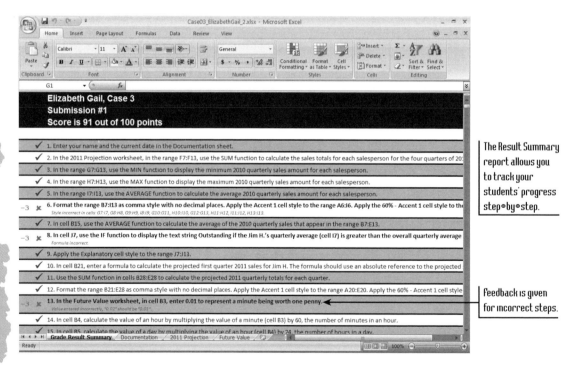

The Result Summary report allows you to track your students' progress step-by-step.

Feedback is given for incorrect steps.

❖ Access all student results for your class and run reports through the Universal Gradebook. These reports can be exported from the Universal Gradebook in .csv format.

For more detailed instructions on how to set up your class and use CaseGrader 2007, please go to *www.course.com* to see the CaseGrader 2007 Instructor's Guide included in the Instructor Resources for this book. You will need a Thomson Course Technology username and password to access the Instructor Resources, as well as the CaseGrader Web site. If you do not have a password, please contact your sales representative.

CONTENTS

CASE STUDY: NEWLEAF PAPER COMPANY

CaseGrader: Microsoft Office Excel 2007 Casebook with Autograding Technology uses a running case study, the NewLeaf Paper Company, throughout all 12 case-based assignments. In these cases you will meet Michael, the regional manager at the Lackawanna County branch office, and his team of sales representatives and accountants as they use Excel to be more efficient in their business while also meeting the regular reporting requests from the corporate office.

The NewLeaf Paper Company cases do not build on one another—you can use or assign the cases in any order.

In Case 1, you'll calculate employee bonuses based on the branch's sales of laser printer paper, the company's best-selling product.

In Case 2, you'll format and complete a two-year summary analysis of sales for the regional office's laser printing paper products. The report will include a breakdown of sales and revenue for each salesperson and highlight trends over the two-year period.

In Case 3, you'll develop a sales projection for the upcoming year based on the current year's sales and a projected percentage increase. You will also use functions to quantify the value of saving money over time.

In Case 4, you'll use charts and graphs to analyze sales and revenue for the Ultra Premium Paper line.

In Case 5 you'll use tables to organize and summarize 4th quarter stationary sales data to prepare for the regional managers' year-end summit.

In Case 6, you'll work with multiple workbooks and worksheets to develop a report to help the corporate office make an informed decision about a possible expansion of the notebook product line.

In Case 7, you'll process monthly notebook sales and calculate the associated shipping and handling charges, based on shipping method and destination. You will also use lookup tables to provide category and description information about each order.

In Case 8, you'll add validation rules and protect worksheet cells to ensure accurate warehouse data entry. You will also create a macro to correctly and accurately transfer data from the new shipment worksheet to the shipment history worksheet.

In Case 9, you'll create a financial analysis of a proposed major renovation of the shipping and warehouse center to determine the profitability of this potential investment.

In Case 10, you'll perform some what-if analysis on a potential new product line, including modeling expected revenue, expenses and net income. You will also use Goal Seek and Scenario Manager to provide a brief summary of the relevant data.

In Case 11, you'll import important NewLeaf company data from a text file, a database, a web page and an XML file (including using an XML map) into Excel. You will also filter, sort, and query the data that you import.

In Case 12, you'll use Visual Basic for Applications (VBA) to verify that new order data entry is accurate and complete. You'll also write a macro that uses an If-Then-ElseIf control structure to calculate overtime pay when it's warranted.

NEWLEAF PAPER COMPANY: CALCULATING EMPLOYEE BONUSES

SKILLS

- ❖ Enter text and dates in cells
- ❖ Select and move a range
- ❖ Insert a row
- ❖ Change a column width
- ❖ Enter numbers in cells
- ❖ Enter formulas in cells
- ❖ Edit cell contents
- ❖ Use the Spelling Checker
- ❖ Insert, rename, delete, and move worksheets

CASE SCENARIO

Michael is the regional manager at the Lackawanna County branch office of the NewLeaf Paper Company. One of his responsibilities is to calculate his employees' bonuses. Branch employees receive an annual bonus based on their branch's sales of laser printer paper, which is the company's best-selling product. Each regional manager receives a percentage of the revenue generated from laser printer paper to distribute to his or her branch employees. The regional manager deducts a small amount to cover the cost of a holiday party and other year-end activities, but the rest of the money, typically 85%, is distributed to the employees as bonuses. Rather than doing these calculations by hand, Michael uses Excel to determine the 2010 laser printer revenue and then to calculate the average employee bonus.

STUDENT DATA FILE

Case01_*Username*_1 (*Note:* Download your personalized start
   file from casegrader.course.com)

Enter Text and Dates in Cells

1. Open the **Case01_*Username*_1** workbook, and then rename the workbook as **Case01_*Username*_2**. In the Documentation sheet, verify your name is in cell B4, and then enter the current date in cell B5.

Select and Move a Range

2. In the Laser Paper worksheet, move the contents of range G13:H14 to range F2:G3.

Insert a Row and Change Column Width

3. Insert a new row at row 7. In the new row, enter the data shown in Figure 1-1.

FIGURE 1-1   Data for new row 7

Cell	Data
A7	LP24289
B7	Heavyweight Laser Printing Paper
C7	7.74

4. Increase the width of column B so that each description fits in the column.

Enter Numbers in Cells

5. In the range D6:D10, enter the data shown in Figure 1-2.

FIGURE 1-2   Data for Laser Paper worksheet

Cell	Data
D6	56301
D7	52582
D8	44505
D9	41842
D10	36135

Enter Formulas in Cells

6. In cell E6, enter a formula to calculate the 2010 revenue for Standard Laser Printing Paper. (*Hint:* Multiply Ream Price by Reams Sold.) Then, enter similar formulas in the range E7:E10 to calculate the 2010 revenue for the remaining laser printer paper types. (*Hint:* You can use copy and paste or AutoFill to enter the formulas in the range E7:E10.)

7. In cell D12, enter the label **TOTAL**.

8. In cell E12, enter a formula to add the total revenue for 2010 sales of laser printer paper.

Edit Cell Contents and Use the Spelling Checker

9. Edit the contents of cell B5 to **Paper Description**.

10. Use the Spelling Checker to find and correct any spelling errors in the Laser Paper worksheet. Ignore the spelling of the company name. Your Laser Paper worksheet should look similar to Figure 1-3.

FIGURE 1-3   Completed Laser Paper worksheet

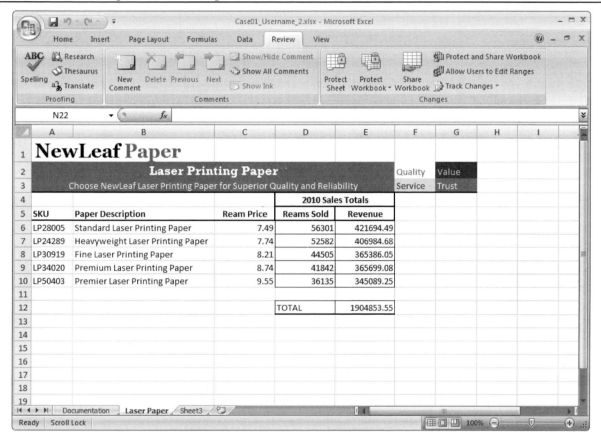

Insert, Rename, Delete, and Move Worksheets

11. Insert a new worksheet in the workbook, and then rename the new Sheet1 worksheet as **Employee Bonus**.

12. Increase the width of column A to be at least 40 characters. Increase the width of column B to be at least 13 characters.

13. In the Employee Bonus worksheet, enter the data shown in Figure 1-4.

FIGURE 1-4   Data for Employee Bonus worksheet

Cell	Data
A1	Total revenue
A2	Branch bonus rate
A3	Total branch bonus
A4	Total bonus for employees
A5	Number of employees at local branch
A6	Average individual bonus for each employee

14. In cell B1 in the Employee Bonus worksheet, enter the value displayed in cell E12 of the Laser Paper worksheet.

15. In cell B2 in the Employee Bonus worksheet, enter **1.25%** as the branch bonus rate. (*Hint:* If you include the percent symbol, %, Excel will understand that you are entering a percent value.)

16. In cell B3, calculate the total branch bonus by multiplying total revenue (cell B1) by branch bonus rate (cell B2).

17. In cell B4, calculate the total bonus for employees by multiplying the total branch bonus (cell B3) by 85%.

18. In cell B5, enter **15** as the number of employees at the local branch.

19. In cell B6, enter a formula to calculate the individual bonus for each employee by dividing the total bonus for employees (cell B4) by the number of employees at the local branch (cell B5). Your Employee Bonus worksheet should look similar to Figure 1-5.

FIGURE 1-5   Completed Employee Bonus worksheet

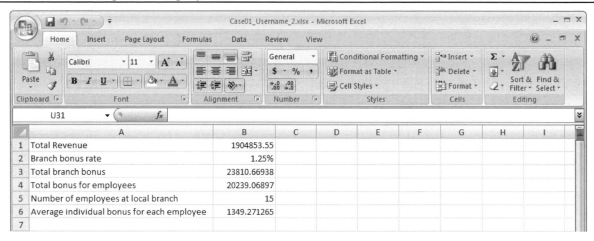

20. Delete the Sheet3 worksheet.

21. Move the Documentation worksheet so it appears after the Laser Paper and Employee Bonus worksheets.

NEWLEAF PAPER COMPANY: FORMATTING A TWO-YEAR ANALYSIS REPORT

SKILLS

- ❖ Change font type, size, style, and color
- ❖ Merge cell ranges
- ❖ Add a cell border
- ❖ Add a fill color
- ❖ Format numbers
- ❖ Change cell alignment
- ❖ Apply cell styles
- ❖ Apply a theme
- ❖ Add conditional formatting with data bars and cell highlighting
- ❖ Change page orientation
- ❖ Add a footer

CASE SCENARIO

The NewLeaf Paper Company's corporate office has requested that each regional office provide a two-year summary analysis of sales for the company's flagship series of Laser Printing Paper products. The summary analysis should include a two-year summary of sales and revenue for each salesperson in the office, and the report should highlight trends over the two-year period. Michael, the Lackawanna office regional manager, needs to compile this summary information and analysis. Under Michael's unorthodox yet effective leadership, the Lackawanna office has proven to be an environment where creativity and energy abound. Though not always "by the book," the Lackawanna team manages to consistently deliver strong sales for NewLeaf products, including the Laser Printing Paper products. Michael has created a workbook to illustrate these points. Now, Michael wants to format his report to include visual appeal that will help draw attention to himself and his team.

STUDENT DATA FILE

Case02_*Username*_1 (*Note:* Download your personalized start file from casegrader.course.com)

Change Font Type, Size, Style, and Color

1. Open the **Case02_Username_1** workbook, and then rename the workbook as **Case02_Username_2**. In the Documentation sheet, verify your name is in cell B4, and then enter the current date in cell B5.

2. In the Yearly Comparison worksheet, format the text in cell A1 as 22-point, bold font.

3. In cell A1, change the font color of the text string "Paper" to Olive Green, Accent 3 from the Theme Colors. The text "NewLeaf" is still black; only "Paper" is olive green. (*Hint:* If Olive Green, Accent 3 is not a Theme Colors option, apply the Office Theme to the worksheet, which will make Olive Green the Accent 3 value.)

Merge Cell Ranges

4. Merge and center the text in cell A3 across the range A3:F3.

5. Merge and center the text in cell A4 across the range A4:F4.

Add a Cell Border and a Fill Color

6. Add the Thick Bottom Border to the merged cell A4.

7. In the range A2:F4, set the fill color to Olive Green, Accent 3 from the Theme Colors and the font color to White, Background 1 from the Theme Colors.

8. Format the text in merged cell A3 as 14-point, bold font.

9. In cell C14, calculate the sum of the 2009 sales for all salespersons. In cell D14, calculate the sum of the 2010 sales of all salespersons.

10. In cell E7, enter the formula =**D7–C7** to calculate the increase in sales for Jim H. from 2009 to 2010. Copy the formula to the range E8:E14.

11. In cell F7, enter the formula =**E7/C7** to calculate the sales percentage increase from 2009 to 2010 for Jim H. Copy the formula to the range F8:F14.

12. In cell C24, calculate the sum of the 2009 revenue for all salespersons. In cell D24, calculate the sum of the 2010 revenue for all salespersons. Enter the appropriate formulas in the range E17:E24 to calculate the revenue increase from 2009 to 2010. (*Hint:* Use a formula similar to the one used in Step 10.) Enter appropriate formulas in the range F17:F24 to calculate the revenue percent increase from 2009 to 2010. (*Hint:* Use a formula similar to the one used in Step 11.)

Format Numbers

13. Format the range C7:E14 as Comma style with no decimal places.

14. Format the range C17:E24 with the Accounting number format.

15. Format the ranges F7:F14 and F17:F24 as percentages with two decimal places.

Change Cell Alignment

16. Center the text in the ranges C6:F6 and C16:F16.

17. In the range A6:A14, merge and center the cells, rotate the text up, and then middle align the text. Format the range A16:A24 the same way.

18. Reduce the width of column A to 8 characters.

19. Apply the Top and Double Bottom Border to the ranges B14:F14 and B24:F24.

Apply Cell Styles and a Theme

20. Apply the Heading 1 cell style to the merged cell A6 and the merged cell A16.

21. Apply the Accent3 cell style to the ranges B6:F6 and B16:F16.

22. Apply the 20% - Accent3 cell style to the ranges E7:F14 and E17:F24.

23. Apply the Aspect theme to the worksheet. Your Yearly Comparison worksheet should look similar to Figure 2-1.

FIGURE 2-1   Completed Yearly Comparison worksheet

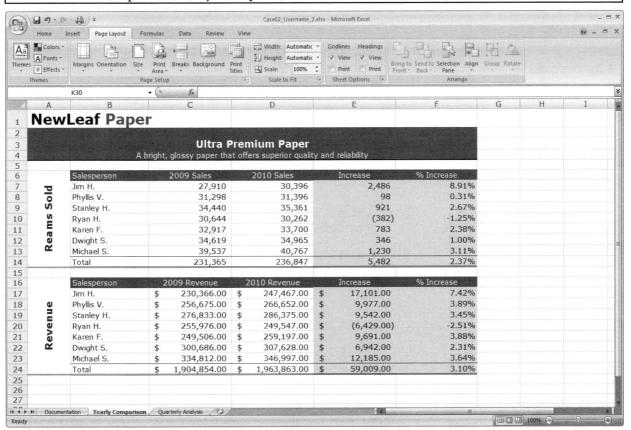

24. In the Quarterly Analysis worksheet, format the ranges C5:J9, C12:J16, and C19:J22 as Comma style with no decimal places.

25. Apply the Top and Thick Bottom Border to the ranges B9:J9 and B16:J16.

26. Apply the Accent5 cell style to the ranges B4:J4, J5:J9, B11:J11, J12:J16, B18:J18, and J19:J22.
27. Apply the 20% - Accent5 cell style to the range B5:B9, B12:B16, and B19:B22.
28. Apply All Borders to the range B19:I22.

Add Conditional Formatting with Data Bars and Cell Highlighting

29. In the range J5:J8, use conditional formatting to apply Green Data Bars. In the range J12:J15, apply Blue Data Bars. Finally, in the range J19:J22, apply Purple Data Bars.
30. In the range C19:I22, use conditional formatting to add a Top/Bottom Rule that formats the Top 10 Items with Green Fill with Dark Green Text.
31. In the range C19:I22, use conditional formatting to add a Top/Bottom Rule that formats the Bottom 10 Items with Light Red Fill with Dark Red Text.

Change Page Orientation and Add a Footer

32. Set the page orientation of the Quarterly Analysis worksheet to Landscape.
33. Add a footer to the Quarterly Analysis worksheet that displays **Visual Is Better** in the right section. Your Quarterly Analysis worksheet should look similar to Figure 2-2.

FIGURE 2-2 Completed Quarterly Analysis worksheet

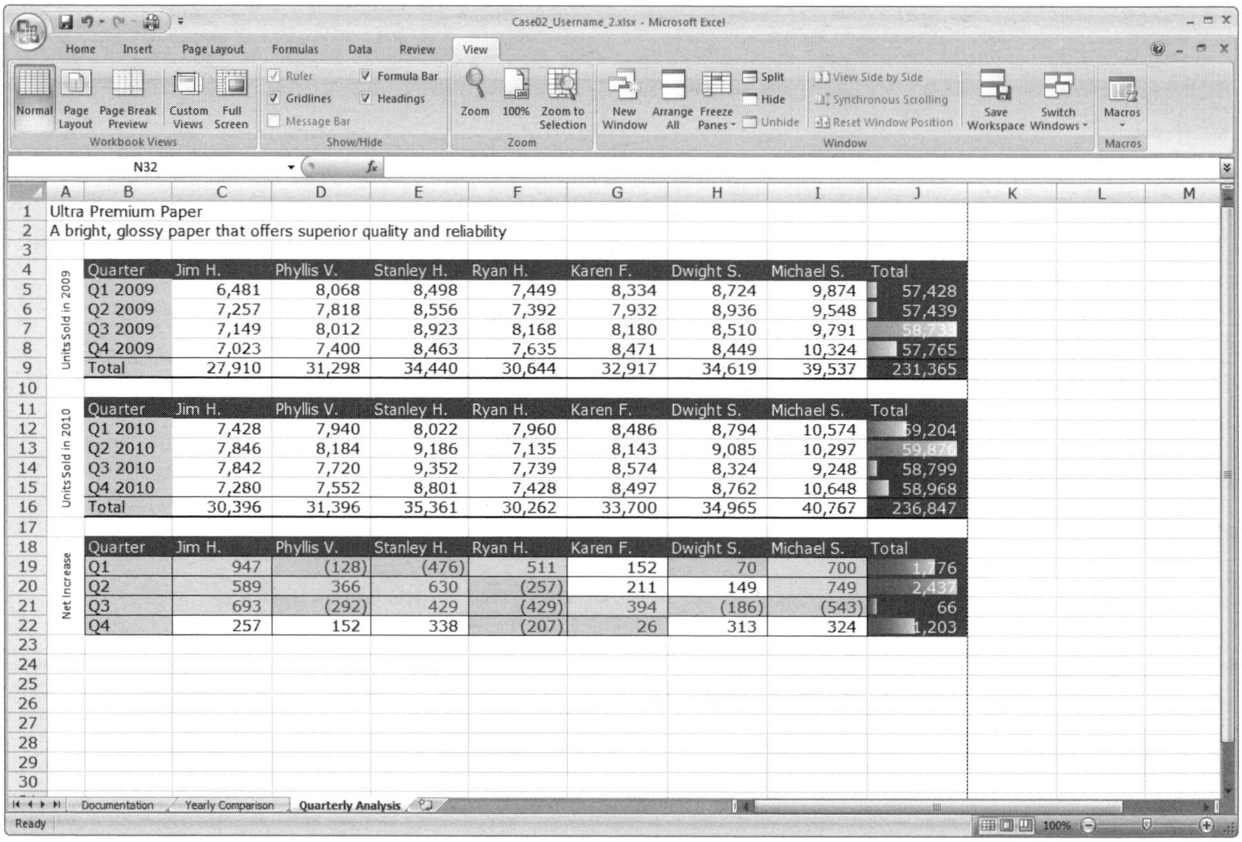

	A	B	C	D	E	F	G	H	I	J
1	Ultra Premium Paper									
2	A bright, glossy paper that offers superior quality and reliability									
3										
4	Units Sold in 2009	Quarter	Jim H.	Phyllis V.	Stanley H.	Ryan H.	Karen F.	Dwight S.	Michael S.	Total
5		Q1 2009	6,481	8,068	8,498	7,449	8,334	8,724	9,874	57,428
6		Q2 2009	7,257	7,818	8,556	7,392	7,932	8,936	9,548	57,439
7		Q3 2009	7,149	8,012	8,923	8,168	8,180	8,510	9,791	58,733
8		Q4 2009	7,023	7,400	8,463	7,635	8,471	8,449	10,324	57,765
9		Total	27,910	31,298	34,440	30,644	32,917	34,619	39,537	231,365
10										
11	Units Sold in 2010	Quarter	Jim H.	Phyllis V.	Stanley H.	Ryan H.	Karen F.	Dwight S.	Michael S.	Total
12		Q1 2010	7,428	7,940	8,022	7,960	8,486	8,794	10,574	59,204
13		Q2 2010	7,846	8,184	9,186	7,135	8,143	9,085	10,297	59,876
14		Q3 2010	7,842	7,720	9,352	7,739	8,574	8,324	9,248	58,799
15		Q4 2010	7,280	7,552	8,801	7,428	8,497	8,762	10,648	58,968
16		Total	30,396	31,396	35,361	30,262	33,700	34,965	40,767	236,847
17										
18	Net Increase	Quarter	Jim H.	Phyllis V.	Stanley H.	Ryan H.	Karen F.	Dwight S.	Michael S.	Total
19		Q1	947	(128)	(476)	511	152	70	700	1,776
20		Q2	589	366	630	(257)	211	149	749	2,437
21		Q3	693	(292)	429	(429)	394	(186)	(543)	66
22		Q4	257	152	338	(207)	26	313	324	1,203

NEWLEAF PAPER COMPANY: PROJECTING 2011 SALES

SKILLS

❖ Use the TODAY function

❖ Use the SUM, MIN, MAX, and AVERAGE functions

❖ Use the IF function

❖ Copy formulas using absolute references

❖ Use the FV function

❖ Use AutoFill to complete a series

CASE SCENARIO

Michael needs to create next year's sales projections for the corporate office. His report will include 2010 sales data along with a projected percentage increase and associated 2011 projected sales. All sales projections reference the projected sales increase value so that changing the one value updates the entire 2011 sales projection. Michael delegates creating the workbook to Jim and then calls the entire staff into the conference room for a motivational talk. Michael begins, "As some famous dead guy once said, 'Time is money.' If that is true, then you can also say that money is time." Michael continues to explain that time is an investment, and every minute matters, just as every penny matters. Jim is intrigued by the idea that time is money and wonders exactly how much money time is worth. To help quantify this idea, Jim uses the Future Value function to determine the future value of saving one penny every minute. Jim designs his workbook to be flexible and able to project the future value of saving a penny every minute for any number of years. Jim also realizes that if the penny a minute were somehow invested, the future value would be even greater. His workbook includes future value calculations for different interest rates.

STUDENT DATA FILE

Case03_*Username*_1 (*Note:* Download your personalized start file from casegrader.course.com)

Use the TODAY Function

1. Open the **Case03_*Username*_1** workbook, and then rename the workbook as **Case03_*Username*_2**. In the Documentation sheet, verify your name is in cell B4, and then enter the current date in cell B5 using the TODAY function.

Use the SUM, MIN, MAX, and AVERAGE Functions

2. In the 2011 Projection worksheet, in the range F7:F13, use the SUM function to calculate the sales totals for each salesperson for the four quarters of 2010.

3. In the range G7:G13, use the MIN function to display the minimum 2010 quarterly sales amount for each salesperson.

4. In the range H7:H13, use the MAX function to display the maximum 2010 quarterly sales amount for each salesperson.

5. In the range I7:I13, use the AVERAGE function to calculate the average 2010 quarterly sales amount for each salesperson.

6. Format the range B7:I13 as comma style with no decimal places. Apply the Accent 1 cell style to the range A6:I6. Apply the 60% - Accent 1 cell style to the range F7:I13. Apply the Heading 4 cell style to cell A5.

7. In cell B15, use the AVERAGE function to calculate the average of the 2010 quarterly sales that appear in the range B7:E13.

Use the IF Function and Copy Formulas Using Absolute References

8. In cell J7, use the IF function to display the text string **Outstanding** if Jim H.'s quarterly average (cell I7) is greater than the overall quarterly average (cell B15), and **Good** otherwise. In the formula in cell J7, use absolute references as appropriate, and then copy the formula to the range J8:J13.

9. Apply the Explanatory cell style to the range J7:J13.

10. In cell B21, enter a formula to calculate the projected first quarter 2011 sales for Jim H. The formula should use an absolute reference to the projected sales increase value in cell B17. (*Hint:* Because sales are projected to increase, the projected 2011 value in cell B21 should be greater than the corresponding 2010 data in cell B7.) Then, calculate the projected sales for all salespersons for all quarters in 2011 by copying the formula in cell B21 to the range B21:E27.

11. Use the SUM function in cells B28:E28 to calculate the projected 2011 quarterly totals for each quarter.

12. Format the range B21:E28 as Comma style with no decimal places. Apply the Accent 1 cell style to the range A20:E20. Apply the 60% - Accent 1 cell style to the range B28:E28. Apply the Heading 4 cell style to cell A19. Your 2011 Projection worksheet should look similar to Figure 3-1.

FIGURE 3-1 Completed 2011 Projection worksheet

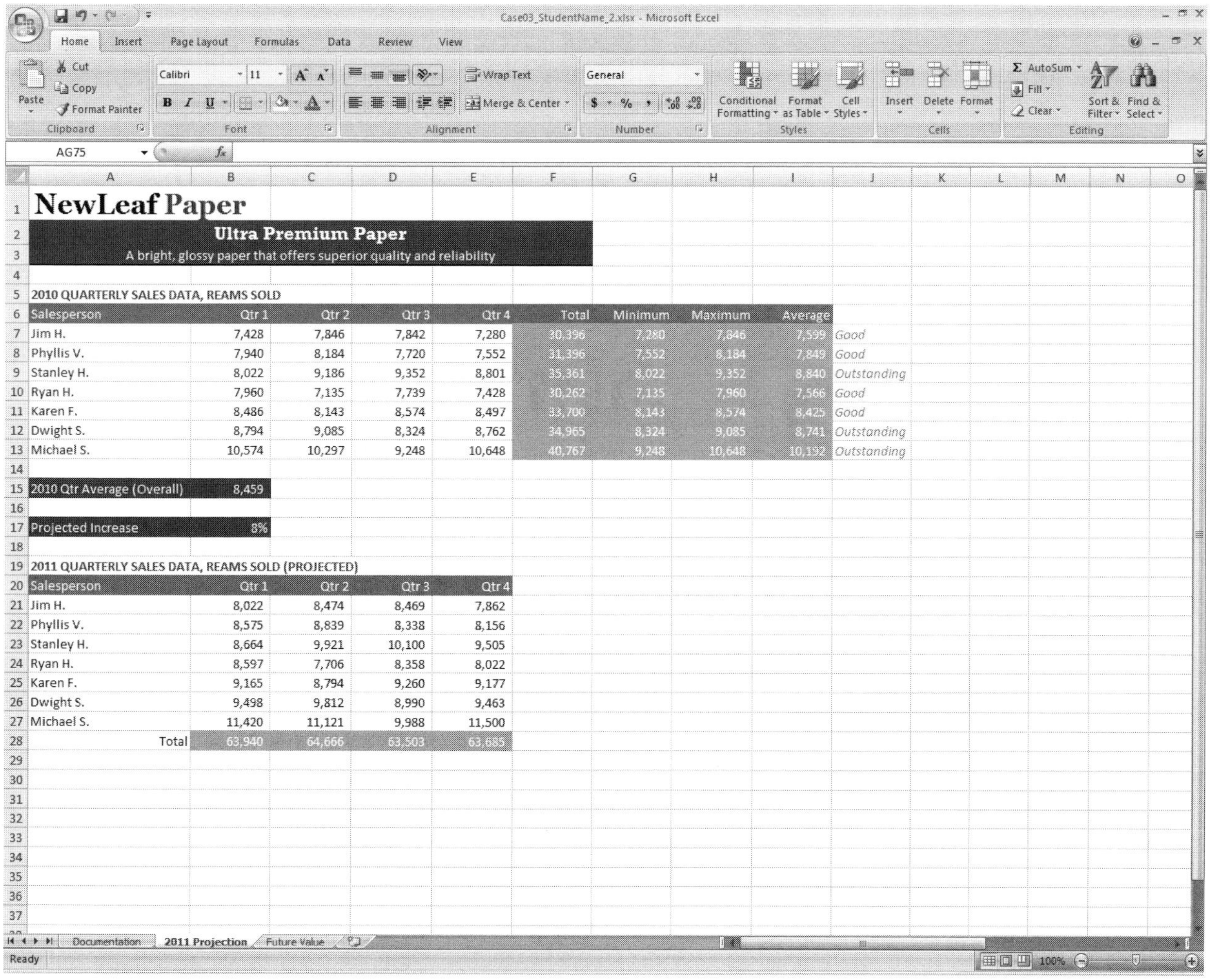

NewLeaf Paper

Ultra Premium Paper

A bright, glossy paper that offers superior quality and reliability

2010 QUARTERLY SALES DATA, REAMS SOLD

Salesperson	Qtr 1	Qtr 2	Qtr 3	Qtr 4	Total	Minimum	Maximum	Average	
Jim H.	7,428	7,846	7,842	7,280	30,396	7,280	7,846	7,599	Good
Phyllis V.	7,940	8,184	7,720	7,552	31,396	7,552	8,184	7,849	Good
Stanley H.	8,022	9,186	9,352	8,801	35,361	8,022	9,352	8,840	Outstanding
Ryan H.	7,960	7,135	7,739	7,428	30,262	7,135	7,960	7,566	Good
Karen F.	8,486	8,143	8,574	8,497	33,700	8,143	8,574	8,425	Good
Dwight S.	8,794	9,085	8,324	8,762	34,965	8,324	9,085	8,741	Outstanding
Michael S.	10,574	10,297	9,248	10,648	40,767	9,248	10,648	10,192	Outstanding

2010 Qtr Average (Overall)	8,459
Projected Increase	8%

2011 QUARTERLY SALES DATA, REAMS SOLD (PROJECTED)

Salesperson	Qtr 1	Qtr 2	Qtr 3	Qtr 4
Jim H.	8,022	8,474	8,469	7,862
Phyllis V.	8,575	8,839	8,338	8,156
Stanley H.	8,664	9,921	10,100	9,505
Ryan H.	8,597	7,706	8,358	8,022
Karen F.	9,165	8,794	9,260	9,177
Dwight S.	9,498	9,812	8,990	9,463
Michael S.	11,420	11,121	9,988	11,500
Total	63,940	64,666	63,503	63,685

Use the FV Function

13. In the Future Value worksheet, in cell B3, enter **0.01** to represent a minute being worth one penny.
14. In cell B4, calculate the value of an hour by multiplying the value of a minute (cell B3) by **60**, the number of minutes in an hour.
15. In cell B5, calculate the value of a day by multiplying the value of an hour (cell B4) by **24**, the number of hours in a day.
16. In cell B6, calculate the value of a month by multiplying the value of a day (cell B5) by **30.4**. (The value 30.4 is a close approximation for the number of days in a month.)
17. Format the range B3:B6 in the Accounting number format.
18. In cell B8, enter a number between **1** and **40** to indicate the number of years you want to save a penny a minute.
19. In cell B9, calculate the number of months (i.e., periods) by multiplying the number of years (cell B8) times **12**.

Use AutoFill to Complete a Series

20. In cell B11, enter the APR value of **0%**. In cell C11, enter the APR value of **2%**. Complete the APR value series from 4% to 14% in the range D11:I11. (*Hint:* You can use AutoFill to complete the series.)

21. In cell B12, enter **12** to represent the number of periods per year (monthly).

22. In cell B13, enter a formula that calculates the interest rate per period by dividing the APR (cell B11) by the number of periods (cell B12). In the B13 formula, include absolute references as appropriate, and then copy the formula to the range C13:I13.

23. Format the range B13:I13 to show the numbers as percentages with four decimal places.

24. In cell B14, use the FV function to calculate the future value using the previously generated values for rate (cell B13), number of periods (cell B9), and monthly amount (cell B6). Multiply this result by **–1** to convert the future value to a positive number. In the formula in cell B14, use absolute references as appropriate, and then copy the formula to the range C14:I14.

25. Format the range B14:I14 in the Accounting number format. Your Future Value worksheet should look similar to Figure 3-2.

FIGURE 3-2   Completed Future Value worksheet

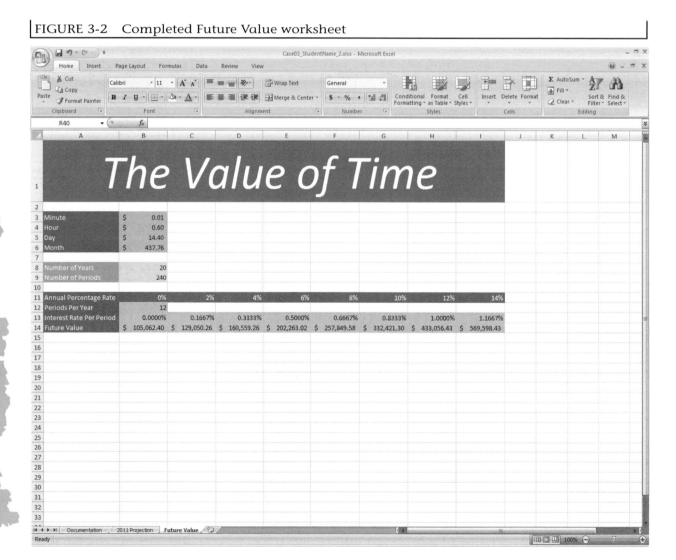

NEWLEAF PAPER COMPANY: CHARTING REVENUE AND SALES PROJECTIONS

SKILLS

- ❖ Create and modify a 3D pie chart
- ❖ Work with chart titles and legends
- ❖ Create and format a column chart
- ❖ Format chart axes
- ❖ Create and format a line chart
- ❖ Create and format a combined chart
- ❖ Work with tick marks and scale values
- ❖ Insert and format a graphic shape

CASE SCENARIO

Angela in Accounting is a big fan of charts. She likes to point out that while numbers can tell a story, a picture can be worth a thousand words—making the story more compelling. Angela needs to present 2010 sales and revenue for the Ultra Premium Paper line to the sales team. She realizes the salespeople will be able to interpret the data more easily if she uses charts. Angela decides to use a 3D pie chart to illustrate how each salesperson contributed to the whole. She also decides to use a column chart to show a side-by-side comparison of each salesperson's relative performance. Angela also wants to show sales trends for the salespeople over time, so she creates a line chart and a combined chart to accomplish this. To maximize the impact of the charts, Angela uses a variety of formatting tools. She also adds a graphic shape to draw attention to a trend in the data.

STUDENT DATA FILE

Case04_*Username*_1 (*Note:* Download your personalized start file from casegrader.course.com)

Create and Modify a 3D Pie Chart

1. Open the **Case04_*Username*_1** file, and then rename the file **Case04_*Username*_2**. In the Documentation sheet, verify your name is in cell B4, and then enter the current date in cell B5.

2. In the Revenue Percentage worksheet, select the range B5:C12, and then create a Pie in 3D chart for the selected range.

3. Move and resize the chart so that the upper-left corner is inside cell D1 and the lower-right corner of the chart is inside cell L17.

4. In the Chart Styles group on the Chart Tools Design tab, open the Chart Styles gallery, and then apply Style 10 to the chart.

5. In the Chart Layouts group on the Chart Tools Design tab, open the Chart Layouts gallery, and then apply Layout 6 to the chart.

6. Change the chart title text to **2010 Revenue Percentages by Employee**.

7. Change the font size of the chart title to 14.

8. Use the Standard Colors category in the Font Color palette to change the font color of the chart title to Blue.

9. Use the Format Chart Area dialog box to change the 3D rotation of the chart. Enter **30** in the X Rotation box and **20** in the Y Rotation box. Your Revenue Percentage worksheet should look similar to Figure 4-1.

> FIGURE 4-1   Completed Revenue Percentage worksheet

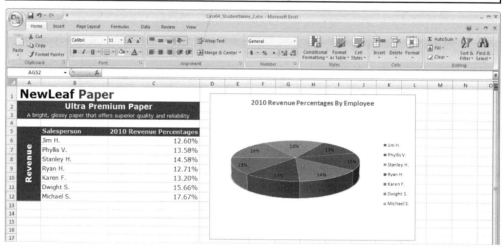

Create and Format a Column Chart

10. In the Revenue Totals worksheet, select the range B5:C12, and then create a Stacked Column in 3D chart for the selected range.

11. Move and resize the chart so that the upper-left corner is inside cell D1 and the lower-right corner of the chart is inside cell K15.

12. Remove the legend from the chart so that it no longer appears and the plot area is resized to fill the available space.

Format Chart Axes

13. Change the font size of the text on the horizontal (category) axis to 12.

14. Change the font size of the text on the vertical (value) axis to 9.

15. Change the Axis Options of the vertical (value) axis so that the Major unit is Fixed and enter the value **75000** for the unit.

16. Add a Primary Horizontal Axis Title below the horizontal axis, with the title text **Salespersons**.

17. Select the data series for the chart, and then open the Format Data Series dialog box. Apply the Gradient fill option and use the default colors and gradient settings. Your Revenue Totals worksheet should look similar to Figure 4-2.

FIGURE 4-2   Completed Revenue Totals worksheet

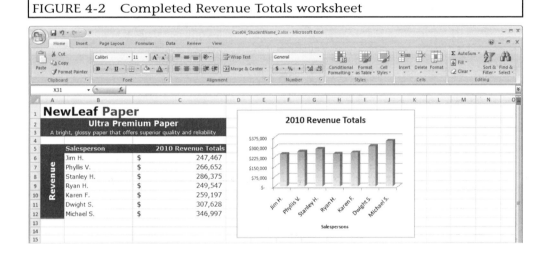

Create and Format a Line Chart

18. In the Daily Sales worksheet, select the range A2:H7, and then create a Line chart for the selected range.

19. Move and resize the chart so that the upper-left corner is inside cell A9 and the lower-right corner of the chart is inside cell I28.

20. Switch the rows and columns in the chart so the days of the week appear on the horizontal axis.

21. Add a Chart Title above the chart with the text **Daily Totals by Salesperson**. Your Daily Sales worksheet should look similar to Figure 4-3.

FIGURE 4-3   Completed Daily Totals chart

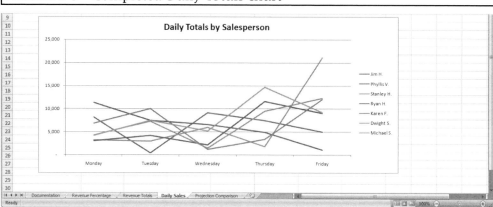

Create and Format a Combined Chart and Work with Tick Marks and Scale Values

22. In the Projection Comparison worksheet, select the range A2:M4, and then create a Clustered Column chart for the selected range.

23. Move and resize the chart so that the upper-left corner is inside cell A6 and the lower-right corner is inside cell M29.

24. Change the Axis Options for the vertical (value) axis so that the Minimum unit is Fixed, with a value of **17000**, and the Major unit is Fixed, with a value of **1000**.

25. In the chart, select the Projected Sales data series, and then change the chart type for this series to Line with Markers.

Insert and Format a Graphic Shape

26. Use the Shapes palette to add a Horizontal Scroll shape (in the Stars and Banners section) to the chart. Add the following text to the shape: **Above Projection 9 months out of 12**. Position the shape in the upper-right area of the chart. Center the text and increase the font size to 24 to make the text easier to read; the text should wrap to a second line before the word **months**. Your Projection Comparison worksheet should look similar to Figure 4-4.

FIGURE 4-4   Completed Projection Comparison chart

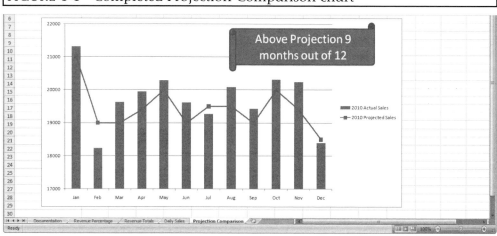

NEWLEAF PAPER COMPANY: END OF YEAR STATIONERY SALES

SKILLS

❖ Enter formulas and functions

❖ Freeze rows and columns

❖ Create a table

❖ Apply conditional formatting

❖ Filter data

❖ Maintain data

❖ Sort table data

❖ Insert subtotals in a table

❖ Create a PivotTable and a PivotChart

CASE SCENARIO

Michael needs to review 4th quarter stationery sales in preparation for a sales presentation he will give at the regional manager's year-end summit. Michael has the basic data (order date, customer ID, salesperson, category, product name, price, and quantity) saved in a workbook. Now he wants to better organize and summarize the data so it's easy to reference and manipulate during his presentation. He needs to complete the worksheet by calculating the total billed for each order (including discounts, as appropriate), creating a table range, and then sorting the table by multiple fields. He plans to use conditional formatting to highlight orders over $120. Michael also wants to create a worksheet that shows subtotals for each salesperson and a worksheet that shows only the November orders, which were higher than expected. In addition, Michael decides to use a PivotTable and PivotChart to visually present the letterhead sales data.

STUDENT DATA FILE

Case05_*Username*_1 (*Note:* Download your personalized start file from casegrader.course.com)

Enter Formulas and Functions

1. Open the **Case05_Username_1** file, and then rename the file **Case05_Username_2**. In the Documentation sheet, verify your name is in cell B4, and then enter the current date in cell B5.

2. On the Stationery Sales worksheet, calculate the amount of each order, placing the result in the Amount column (column H). Use a formula that multiplies the price by the quantity.

3. Calculate the appropriate discount for each order. Use the IF function with an absolute reference to the discount value listed in cell I3. The discount only applies to orders with a quantity of two or more; otherwise, the discount is zero. Place the calculated value in the Discount column (column I).

4. Calculate the total for each order, placing the calculated value in the Total column (column J). Use a formula that subtracts the discount from the amount.

Freeze Rows and Columns

5. Freeze rows and columns in the worksheet so the column headings remain visible as you scroll vertically, and the Order Date and Customer ID columns remain visible as you scroll horizontally.

Create a Table and Apply Conditional Formatting

6. Create a table for the Stationery Sales worksheet. The range for the table should include row 5 as the header row.

7. Add a record with the following information:
   Order Date: **10/19/2010**
   Customer ID: **NLC-19-2610**
   Sales Person: **Ryan H.**
   Category: **Note Card**
   Product Name: **Inspire**
   Unit Price: **$74.90**
   Quantity: **2**

8. Find the record with customer ID of NLC-41-4889, and update the quantity to 3.

9. Delete the record with customer ID of NLC-39-3041.

10. Apply conditional formatting to the Total column. Highlight orders in which the total is greater than $120, using a Yellow Fill with Dark Yellow text.

11. Sort the table by multiple fields: by category from A to Z; within category by product name, from A to Z; and within product name by order date, from oldest to newest. Your Stationery Sales worksheet should look similar to Figure 5-1.

Figure 5-1 Completed Stationery Sales worksheet

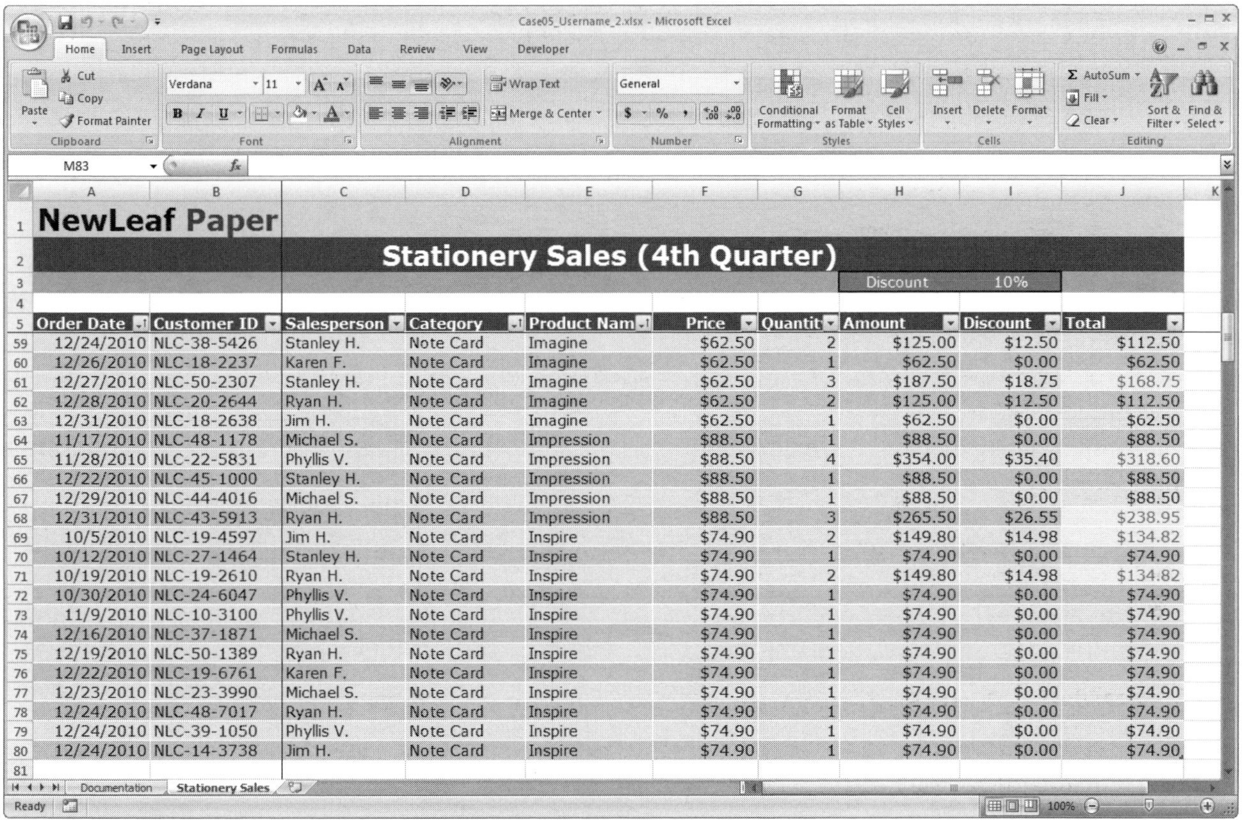

	Order Date	Customer ID	Salesperson	Category	Product Name	Price	Quantity	Amount	Discount	Total
59	12/24/2010	NLC-38-5426	Stanley H.	Note Card	Imagine	$62.50	2	$125.00	$12.50	$112.50
60	12/26/2010	NLC-18-2237	Karen F.	Note Card	Imagine	$62.50	1	$62.50	$0.00	$62.50
61	12/27/2010	NLC-50-2307	Stanley H.	Note Card	Imagine	$62.50	3	$187.50	$18.75	$168.75
62	12/28/2010	NLC-20-2644	Ryan H.	Note Card	Imagine	$62.50	2	$125.00	$12.50	$112.50
63	12/31/2010	NLC-18-2638	Jim H.	Note Card	Imagine	$62.50	1	$62.50	$0.00	$62.50
64	11/17/2010	NLC-48-1178	Michael S.	Note Card	Impression	$88.50	1	$88.50	$0.00	$88.50
65	11/28/2010	NLC-22-5831	Phyllis V.	Note Card	Impression	$88.50	4	$354.00	$35.40	$318.60
66	12/22/2010	NLC-45-1000	Stanley H.	Note Card	Impression	$88.50	1	$88.50	$0.00	$88.50
67	12/29/2010	NLC-44-4016	Michael S.	Note Card	Impression	$88.50	1	$88.50	$0.00	$88.50
68	12/31/2010	NLC-43-5913	Ryan H.	Note Card	Impression	$88.50	3	$265.50	$26.55	$238.95
69	10/5/2010	NLC-19-4597	Jim H.	Note Card	Inspire	$74.90	2	$149.80	$14.98	$134.82
70	10/12/2010	NLC-27-1464	Stanley H.	Note Card	Inspire	$74.90	1	$74.90	$0.00	$74.90
71	10/19/2010	NLC-19-2610	Ryan H.	Note Card	Inspire	$74.90	2	$149.80	$14.98	$134.82
72	10/30/2010	NLC-24-6047	Phyllis V.	Note Card	Inspire	$74.90	1	$74.90	$0.00	$74.90
73	11/9/2010	NLC-10-3100	Phyllis V.	Note Card	Inspire	$74.90	1	$74.90	$0.00	$74.90
74	12/16/2010	NLC-37-1871	Michael S.	Note Card	Inspire	$74.90	1	$74.90	$0.00	$74.90
75	12/19/2010	NLC-50-1389	Ryan H.	Note Card	Inspire	$74.90	1	$74.90	$0.00	$74.90
76	12/22/2010	NLC-19-6761	Karen F.	Note Card	Inspire	$74.90	1	$74.90	$0.00	$74.90
77	12/23/2010	NLC-23-3990	Michael S.	Note Card	Inspire	$74.90	1	$74.90	$0.00	$74.90
78	12/24/2010	NLC-48-7017	Ryan H.	Note Card	Inspire	$74.90	1	$74.90	$0.00	$74.90
79	12/24/2010	NLC-39-1050	Phyllis V.	Note Card	Inspire	$74.90	1	$74.90	$0.00	$74.90
80	12/24/2010	NLC-14-3738	Jim H.	Note Card	Inspire	$74.90	1	$74.90	$0.00	$74.90

Filter Data and Add a Total Row

12. Create a copy of the Stationery Sales worksheet. Rename the new worksheet as **AutoFilter**.
13. In the AutoFilter worksheet, use a filter to display only those orders from November.
14. Add a Total Row to the filtered table. Your AutoFilter worksheet should look similar to Figure 5-2.

Figure 5-2   Completed AutoFilter worksheet

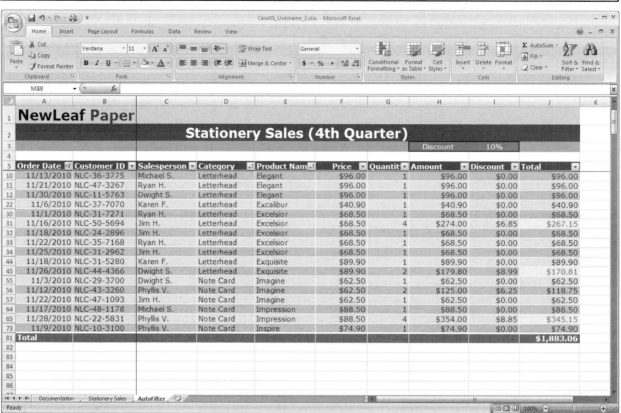

Sort Table Data and Insert Subtotals

15. Create another copy of the Stationery Sales worksheet. Rename the copied worksheet as **Subtotals**.

16. Sort the list in ascending order by salesperson.

17. Convert the table to a normal range, and then use the Subtotal command to sum the sales total for each salesperson. Your Subtotals worksheet should look similar to Figure 5-3.

Figure 5-3   Completed Subtotals worksheet

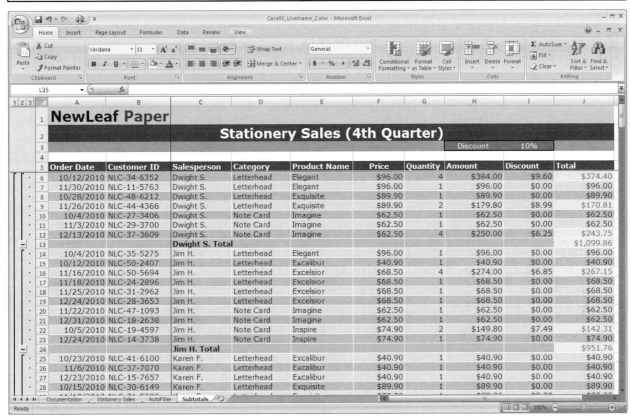

Create a PivotTable and a PivotChart

18. Return to the Stationery Sales worksheet. Create a PivotTable, using the orders table, and place the PivotTable in a new worksheet. Rename the new sheet as **PivotTable and PivotChart**.

19. Lay out the PivotTable to show totals by product name and salesperson. Use Product Name as the row field, Sales Person as the column field, and Sum of Total as the values.

20. Format the data items as Currency. Resize the columns as necessary so the column widths are wide enough to show the currency formatted data items.

21. Format the PivotTable using Pivot Style Medium 2.

22. Create a PivotChart based on the PivotTable. Use the Stacked Column in 3-D chart type. Move the chart so it appears below the PivotTable.

23. Filter the Chart so that only the four letterhead products (Elegant, Excalibur, Excelsior, and Exquisite) are displayed. Your PivotTable and PivotChart worksheet should look similar to Figure 5-4.

Figure 5-4   Completed PivotTable and PivotChart worksheet

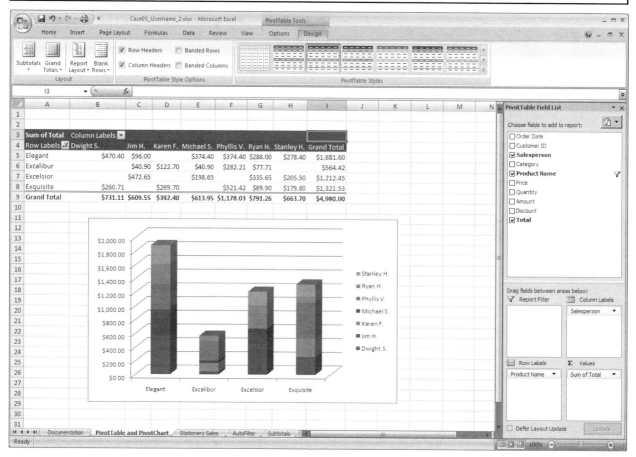

NEWLEAF PAPER COMPANY: TRACKING NOTEBOOK SALES

SKILLS

- ❖ Edit and format multiple worksheets at the same time

- ❖ Create cell references to other worksheets

- ❖ Change the page setup in a worksheet group

- ❖ Consolidate information from multiple worksheets using 3D references

- ❖ Create a link to data in another workbook

- ❖ Insert a hyperlink in a cell

- ❖ Create an Excel workspace

- ❖ Create a static Web page

- ❖ Create a custom template

CASE SCENARIO

Notebook products are a small but reliable sales performer for the NewLeaf Paper Company. The marketing team at company headquarters is considering expanding this product line to include a greater variety of notebook sizes and styles. To prepare for a product development meeting, each regional manager has been asked to submit a quarterly sales summary of notebook products. Michael has a workbook containing notebook sales for the Lackawanna office on four worksheets, one for each quarter. To prepare the workbook for the meeting, he needs to add totals to the quarterly information, summarize data from the four quarters and also from the previous year's notebook sales summary, and format the data so it's easier to read. Michael also decides to post a Web page of the Q4 worksheet on the company intranet as an example to which other regional managers can refer. The marketing team has also been charged with re-evaluating the order process as part of this effort, so Michael decides to include a link to the order form his branch uses and to provide the form as a template other branches can customize for their purposes.

STUDENT DATA FILE

Case06_*Username*_Template.xltx

Case06_2009.xlsx

Case06_OrderForm.xlsx

(*Note*: Download these start files from casegrader.course.com)

Edit and Format Multiple Worksheets at the Same Time

1. Create a new workbook from the **Case06_*Username*_Template.xltx** template, and then save the file as **Case06_*Username*_2**. (*Hint*: Save the new workbook with the file type *.xlsx.) In the Documentation sheet, verify your name is in cell B4, and then enter the current date in cell B5.

2. In cell G4 of the Q1 through Q4 worksheets, enter a formula to calculate gross sales by multiplying units sold by unit price. Then copy the formula to the range G5:G18. (*Hint*: First group the Q1 through Q4 worksheets.)

3. In cell G19 of the Q1 through Q4 worksheets, enter a formula to calculate the total gross sales for each respective worksheet.

4. Apply the Currency format to the range F4:G19 in the grouped Q1 through Q4 worksheets. (*Hint*: Ungroup the Q1 through Q4 worksheets when you are finished.)

Create Cell References to Other Worksheets

5. In cell B5 of the Q2 worksheet only, enter a formula that adds the total gross sales for the first quarter (cell B5 in the Q1 worksheet) and the total gross sales for the current quarter (cell G19 in the Q2 worksheet). (*Hint*: Use the point-and-click method to enter the Q1 cell reference in the formula.)

6. In cell B5 of the Q3 worksheet, enter a formula that adds the total gross sales for the previous quarters (cell B5 in the Q2 worksheet) and the total gross sales for the current quarter (cell G19 in the Q3 worksheet).

7. In cell B5 of the Q4 worksheet, enter a formula that adds the total gross sales for the previous quarters (cell B5 in the Q3 worksheet) and the total gross sales for the current quarter (cell G19 in the Q4 worksheet). Your Q4 worksheet should look similar to Figure 6-1.

FIGURE 6-1   Completed Q4 worksheet

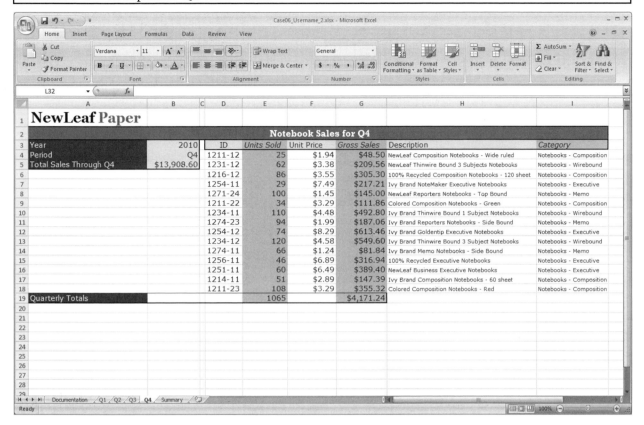

Change the Page Setup in a Worksheet Group

8. For the Q1 through Q4 worksheets, change the page setup so each page is centered horizontally and vertically.

Consolidate Information from Multiple Worksheets Using 3D References

9. In cell B4 of the Summary worksheet, calculate the total units sold in 2010 by entering a SUM function formula with a 3D reference to cell E19 in the Q1 through Q4 worksheets.

Create a Link to Data in Another Workbook

10. In cell B5 of the Summary worksheet, create a workbook reference to the Total Units Sold in 2009 value in cell B4 of the Summary worksheet in the Case06_2009 workbook. (*Hint*: First open the Case06_2009 workbook, which contains the summary information for 2009 notebook sales.)

11. In cell B6 of the Summary worksheet, determine the 2010 Net Annual Increase by calculating 2010 units sold (B4) minus 2009 units sold (B5).

12. In cell B7 of the Summary worksheet, determine the 2010 Percent Growth by calculating the net annual increase (B6) divided by the 2009 units sold (B5).

Insert a Hyperlink in a Cell

13. In cell A10 of the Summary worksheet, insert a hyperlink to the **Case06_OrderForm** workbook. Set the text that displays for the link to **Link to Order Form**. Your Summary worksheet should look similar to Figure 6-2.

FIGURE 6-2   Completed Summary worksheet

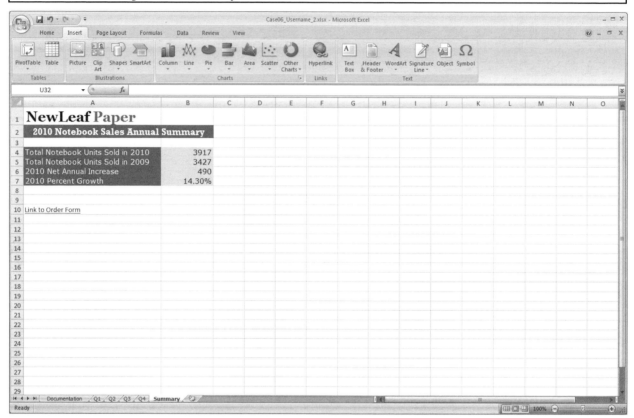

Create an Excel Workspace

14. With both the **Case06_Username_2** and **Case06_2009** files open, place the two workbooks in a tiled layout and then create a workspace named **Case06_Workspace.xlw**.

Create a Static Web Page

15. Save the Q4 worksheet as a Single File Web Page named **Q4.mht**, changing the title to **Q4 Notebook Sales**. Publish the page and then view it in a Web browser. Your Web page should look similar to Figure 6-3.

FIGURE 6-3   Web browser view of Q4.mht

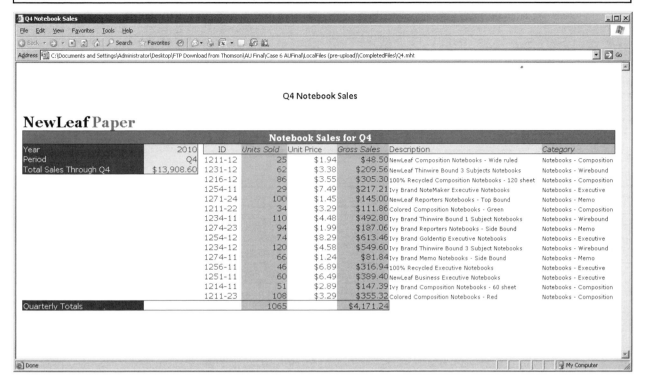

Create a Custom Template

16. Save and close the **Case06_Username_2** workbook, open the **Case06_OrderForm** workbook, and then save the workbook as a template named **Case06_OrderForm.xltx**.
(*Hint*: First change the file type, and then browse to the folder in which you want to
save the file.)

NOTE: Students will submit the following files for grading:

❖ Case06_Username_2.xlsx

❖ Case06_Workspace.xlw

❖ Q4.mht

❖ Case06_OrderForm.xltx

NEWLEAF PAPER COMPANY: TRACKING EXPENSES

SKILLS

- ❖ Use Named Tables and Calculated Columns
- ❖ Use Nested IF functions
- ❖ Use the AND function
- ❖ Use the VLOOKUP function
- ❖ Summarize data using the COUNTIF function
- ❖ Summarize data using the SUMIF function
- ❖ Summarize data using the AVERAGEIF function
- ❖ Summarize data using database functions

CASE SCENARIO

Michael is processing January notebook sales and needs to calculate shipping and handling charges. The workbook he has created includes a sheet listing the date of each sale, unit ID, units sold, unit price, and gross sales. The sheet also lists whether the customer selected priority or standard shipping and whether the mailing address is in state or not. Michael needs to complete the worksheet by calculating the shipping and handling for each order and determining what type of packing the package will receive (based on shipping method and destination). He would also like to include category and description information about each order, which is available in a lookup table in another sheet in the workbook. Finally, he wants to provide summary sales data in a separate worksheet for later review.

STUDENT DATA FILE

Case07_*Username*_1 (*Note:* Download your personalized start file from casegrader.course.com)

1. Open the **Case07_*Username*_1** file, and then rename the file **Case07_*Username*_2**. In the Documentation sheet, verify your name is in cell B4, and then enter the current date in cell B5.

Use Named Tables and Calculated Columns

2. In the January Sales worksheet, select cell A4 and create a table with headers that spans the range A4:K50. Name the table **January**.

Use Nested IF Functions

3. In the S&H column, enter a nested condition to determine shipping and handling, based on the following criteria: If Shipping is Priority (or P) then the S&H value is 12.75; otherwise, if Shipping is Not in State (or N) then the S&H value is 7.25; otherwise, the S&H value is 5.45. Use the calculated columns **Shipping** and **In State** in your nested condition, which will look similar to =IF([Shipping]="P",12.75,IF([In State]="N",7.25,5.45))

Use the AND Function

4. In the January table's Packing column, enter a condition that displays the value **Double** if the order is more than 9 units sold AND the order is not in state. Use the calculated columns **Units Sold** and **In State** in your condition, which will look similar to =IF(AND([Units Sold]>9,[In State]="N"),"Double","Single")

Use the VLOOKUP Function

5. In cell J5, use the VLOOKUP function to display the appropriate description for the order. Use the book ID as the lookup value. The lookup table is the table named **Description** in the Lookup Tables worksheet; the column index number is 2, and the range_lookup value is FALSE.

6. In cell K5, use the VLOOKUP function to display the appropriate category name. Use the book ID as the lookup value. The lookup table is the table named **Category** in the Lookup Tables worksheet, and the column index number is 2. When specifying the range_lookup value, remember that you are referencing a table containing ranges of ID values, so you want an approximate match.

7. Resize the width of column A to be less than 11 characters. Your January Sales worksheet should look similar to Figure 7-1.

FIGURE 7-1   Completed January Sales worksheet

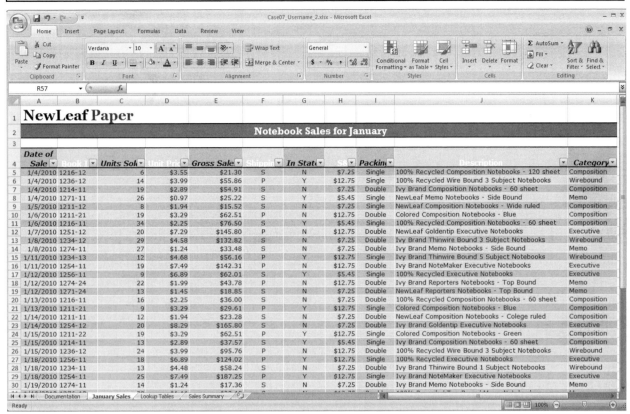

Summarize Data Using the COUNTIF Function

8. In cell C6 of the Sales Summary worksheet, use the COUNTIF function to enter a formula that counts all the January sales of Composition notebooks. For the range, use the Category column in the January table. The formula will look similar to =COUNTIF(January[Category], B6) or =COUNTIF(January[Category], "Composition")

9. Use the COUNTIF function to enter a formula in cell C7 to count the January sales of Wirebound notebooks. Use the COUNTIF function to enter a formula in cell C8 to count the January sales of Executive notebooks. Use the COUNTIF function to enter a formula in cell C9 to count the January sales of Memo notebooks. (*Hint*: If you chose the right formula for cell C6, you can just copy that formula into cells C7, C8, and C9.)

Summarize Data Using the SUMIF Function

10. Use the SUMIF function in cells D6, D7, D8, and D9 to sum the January sales of Composition, Wirebound, Executive, and Memo notebooks, respectively.

Summarize Data Using the AVERAGEIF Function

11. Use the AVERAGEIF function in cells E6, E7, E8, and E9 to average the January sales of Composition, Wirebound, Executive, and Memo notebooks, respectively.

Summarize Data using Database Functions

12. Enter the criteria values as shown in Figure 7-2.

FIGURE 7-2   Data for category criteria

Cell	Data
G17	P
H17	Y
J17	P
K17	N
G21	S
H21	Y
J21	S
K21	N

13. Use the DSUM function in cell C14 to calculate the total gross sales of all January sales that satisfy the criteria in the range G16:H17. For the database, use **January[#All]** with the field "Gross Sales". The formula will look similar to =DSUM(January[#All], "Gross Sales",G16:H17)

14. Use the DSUM function in cells D14, C15, and D15 to calculate total gross sales of all January sales that satisfy the criteria in the ranges J16:K17, G20:H21, and J20:K21, respectively.

15. Use the DAVERAGE function in cells C20, D20, C21, and D21 to calculate the average gross sale of all January sales that satisfy the criteria in the ranges G16:H17, J16:K17, G20:H21, and J20:K21, respectively.

16. Format the ranges D6:E9, C14:D15, and C20:D21 as Currency. Your Sales Summary worksheet should look similar to Figure 7-3.

FIGURE 7-3   Completed Sales Summary worksheet

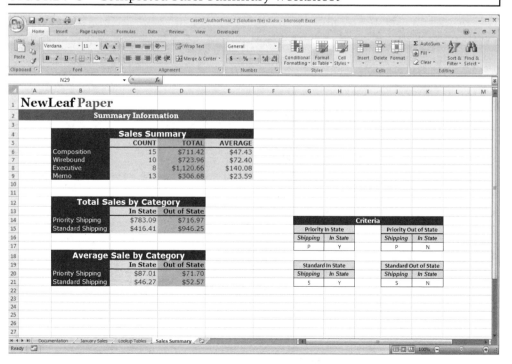

NEWLEAF PAPER COMPANY: VALIDATING INVENTORY DATA

SKILLS

- ❖ Protect a worksheet
- ❖ Create validation rules for data entry
- ❖ Create and use defined names
- ❖ Create a macro using the macro recorder
- ❖ Assign a macro to a button
- ❖ Run a macro

CASE SCENARIO

Kevin from Accounting has just reviewed warehouse inventory reports from last quarter and found numerous errors in the files. He believes the errors occurred during the data entry process when outbound shipments were recorded. To help avoid these data entry errors in the future, Kevin decides to create a worksheet that will first validate the warehouse clerk ID, shipment date, and product ID prior to recording the shipment and updating the shipment history. Furthermore, Kevin decides to protect the workbook so that users can enter data only into certain cells. He also wants to use a macro to accurately transfer data from the shipment entry form to the shipping history worksheet.

STUDENT DATA FILE

Case08_*Username*_1.xlsx (*Note*: Download your personalized start file from casegrader.course.com)

Protect a Worksheet

1. Open the **Case08_*Username*_1** file, and then save the file as an Excel Macro-Enabled Workbook named **Case08_*Username*_2.xlsm**. In the Documentation sheet, verify your name is in cell B4, and then enter the current date in cell B5.

2. Unlock cells B4 and B5, and then protect the Documentation sheet. Do not use a password to enable protection. (*Hint*: To test your sheet protection, try entering data into cells other than those you unlocked.)

Create Validation Rules for Data Entry

3. In the New Shipments worksheet, create a validation rule for cell C3 that allows the user to enter only a whole number between 5000 and 6500.

4. For the validation rule in cell C3, add an input message with the title **Clerk ID** and the input message **Enter the clerk ID**.

5. For the validation rule in cell C3, add an error alert message with a Stop style, the title **Invalid ID**, and an error message **Clerk ID must be between 5000 and 6500**.

6. Create a validation rule in cell C4 that allows the user to enter only a date that is greater than January 1, 2009.

7. For the validation rule in cell C4, add an input message with the title **Date of shipment** and the input message **Enter the date this shipment occurred**.

8. For the validation rule in cell C4, add an error alert with a Stop style, the title **Invalid ship date**, and the error message **Ship date must occur after January 1, 2009**.

9. Create a validation rule in cell C5 that allows the user to select only from the list of values in the range E4:E13. Add an input message with a title and input message of your choice. Add an error alert with a Stop style and a title and error message of your choice.

Create and Use Defined Names

10. Define the name **Cost** for cell C7.

11. Define the name **Units** for cell C8.

12. Enter a formula in cell C9 that multiplies the cell named "Cost" by the cell named "Units." (*Note*: The formula will result in an error, but this will be addressed when you enter data in the following step.)

Create a Macro using the Macro Recorder

13. Enter the data shown in Figure 8-1 in cells C3, C4, C5, and C8 of the New Shipments worksheet.

FIGURE 8-1   Data for first new shipment

Cell	Data
Warehouse Clerk ID	5766
Shipment Date	2/7/2009
Product ID	IX
Units Shipped	100

14. With the New Shipments sheet active, create a macro named **NewShipment** that is stored in this workbook and performs the following tasks:

a. Switches to the Shipment History worksheet, and then inserts a blank record in the fifth row, shifting the rest of the records down. (*Hint*: Leave the fourth row blank.)

b. Switches to the New Shipments worksheet, copies the values in the range C3:C9, switches to the Shipment History worksheet, and then pastes the transposed values into the new blank record in the fifth row. (*Hint*: Use the Paste Special command and select the Values and Transpose options.)

c. Clears the values in cells C3, C4, C5, and C8 of the New Shipments worksheet.

Assign a Macro to a Button

15. Create a macro button in the New Shipments worksheet, assigning the NewShipment macro to the button. Move and resize the button so that the upper-left corner is inside cell C11 and the lower-right corner is inside cell C13.

16. Change the button's default label to **Record New Shipment**. Your New Shipments worksheet should look similar to Figure 8-2. (*Note*: If you right-click on the button, you can edit the text without running the macro. If you accidentally run the macro without having valid data in the input cells, the macro will insert incomplete records into the Shipment History worksheet. If this happens, delete any incomplete records from the Shipment History worksheet. In Case 12 you will write VBA code to avoid adding incomplete records.)

FIGURE 8-2   Completed New Shipments worksheet

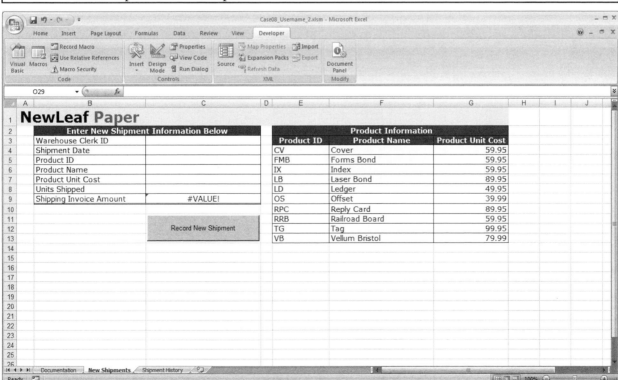

Run a Macro

17. Enter the data shown in Figure 8-3 in cells C3, C4, C5, and C8 of the New Shipments worksheet, and then run the macro using the macro button.

FIGURE 8-3   Data for second new shipment

Cell	Data
Warehouse Clerk ID	6000
Shipment Date	3/1/2009
Product ID	RPC
Units Shipped	50

18. Enter the data shown in Figure 8-4 in cells C3, C4, C5, and C8 of the New Shipments worksheet, and then run the macro using the macro button. Your Shipment History worksheet should look similar to Figure 8-5.

FIGURE 8-4   Data for third new shipment

Cell	Data
Warehouse Clerk ID	5888
Shipment Date	3/3/2009
Product ID	CV
Units Shipped	25

FIGURE 8-5   Completed Shipment History worksheet

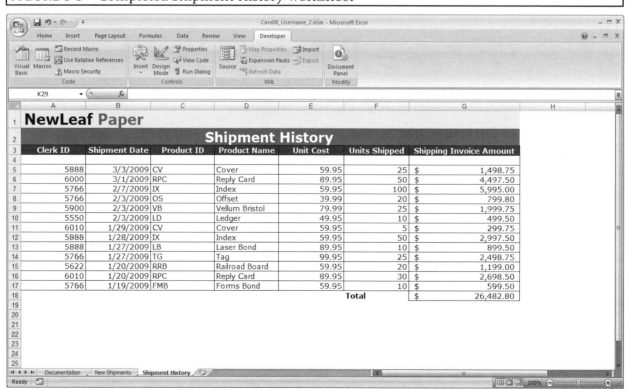

NEWLEAF PAPER COMPANY: PROFITABILITY OF A NEW WAREHOUSE PURCHASE

SKILLS

- ❖ Create an amortization table

- ❖ Calculate a conditional sum

- ❖ Calculate a depreciation schedule

- ❖ Work with an income statement

- ❖ Work with a cash flow statement

- ❖ Work with a balance sheet

- ❖ Determine a payback period

- ❖ Calculate a net present value

- ❖ Calculate an internal rate of return

CASE SCENARIO

NewLeaf corporate headquarters is considering a major renovation of the shipping and warehouse center. It is estimated the project will cost $750,000. To pay for the remodeling, the company would need to take out a five–year loan at 7.5% interest, compounded monthly. Oscar, in Accounting, has been assigned the task of creating a financial analysis of this project to determine the profitability of this potential investment. He estimates that the remodeling will depreciate from $750,000 to a salvage value one-fifth of that in eight years time. Oscar's financial analysis will include a projected income statement worksheet to project the annual income for the next five years, assuming declining balance depreciation. His cash flow statement worksheet will project the company's yearly cash flow for the next five years. The balance sheet worksheet will calculate the five–year projection for assets and liabilities. Finally, Oscar wants to create a summary analysis of the profitability of the investment, assuming at least an 18% rate of return.

STUDENT DATA FILE

Case09_*Username*_1 (*Note:* Download your personalized start file from casegrader.course.com)

1. Open the **Case09_Username_1** file, and then rename the file **Case09_Username_2**. In the Documentation sheet, verify your name is in cell B4, and then enter the current date in cell B5.

Create an Amortization Table and Calculate a Conditional Sum

2. In the Loan Analysis worksheet, enter a formula in cell B7 to calculate the rate per period based on the loan conditions already entered in the worksheet. In cell B8, enter a formula to calculate the number of periods based on the loan conditions already entered in the worksheet. In cell B9, use the PMT function to calculate the total monthly payment on the loan. Assume that the loan will be completely paid off at the end of the last period.

3. Fill in the missing information for the amortization table in the range G4:H23. In cell G4, use the IPMT function to calculate the interest payment for the current payment period. In cell H4, use the PPMT function to calculate the principal payment for the current payment period. Both functions should use a mix of absolute and relative references, as appropriate, so the range G4:H4 can be copied to the cells below. Complete the amortization table by copying the range G4:H4 to cells G23:H23.

4. In the cell range D27:H28, use the SUMIF function to calculate the total interest and principal payments for each of the five years. Your Loan Analysis worksheet should look similar to Figure 9-1.

FIGURE 9-1   Completed Loan Analysis worksheet

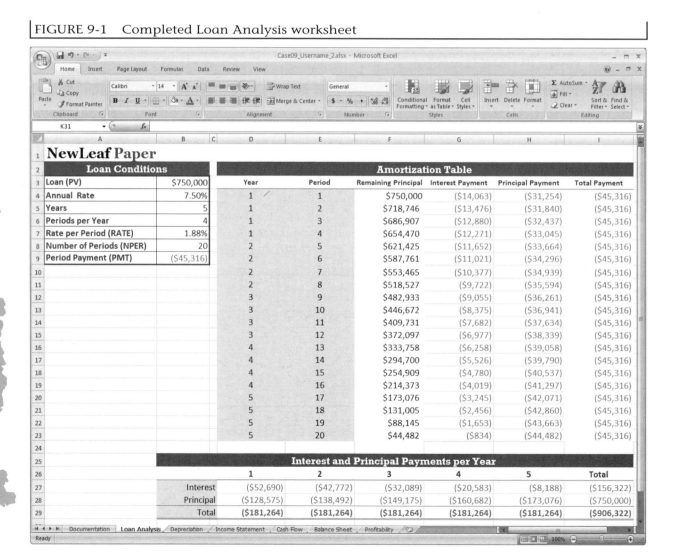

Calculate a Depreciation Schedule

5. In the Depreciation worksheet, display the salvage value in cell B5 by calculating one-fifth of the value in cell B4.

6. In the cell range B10:I10, use the SLN function to calculate the yearly depreciation of the asset, assuming a straight-line depreciation.

7. In the cell range B14:I14, use the DB function to calculate the yearly depreciation of the asset, assuming declining balance depreciation. (*Hint*: This can be accomplished by using the function in cell B14 with an appropriate mix of absolute and relative references, and then copying the formula to cells C14:I14.) Your Depreciation worksheet should look similar to Figure 9-2.

FIGURE 9-2   Completed Depreciation worksheet

Work with an Income Statement

8. In the Income Statement worksheet, project the revenue in years 2 through 4 by interpolating the increase in revenue between Year 1 ($3,500,000) and Year 5 ($5,200,000), assuming a growth trend. The resulting five–year revenue projection should fill the range B7:F7.

9. In cell B20, enter the declining balance depreciation for Year 1 by referencing cell B14 on the Depreciation worksheet. Treat the depreciation as an expense by making it a negative value. Copy this formula into the range C20:F20, to include the first five years of the declining balance depreciation in your projected income statement.

10. In cells B23:F23, enter the yearly interest payments by referencing the range D27:H27 on the Loan Analysis worksheet.

11. In cells B26:F26, calculate the yearly estimated tax using the tax rate in cell F4 times the earnings before taxes for each year. Treat the estimated tax as an expense by making it a negative value. Your Income Statement worksheet should look similar to Figure 9-3.

FIGURE 9-3   Completed Income Statement worksheet

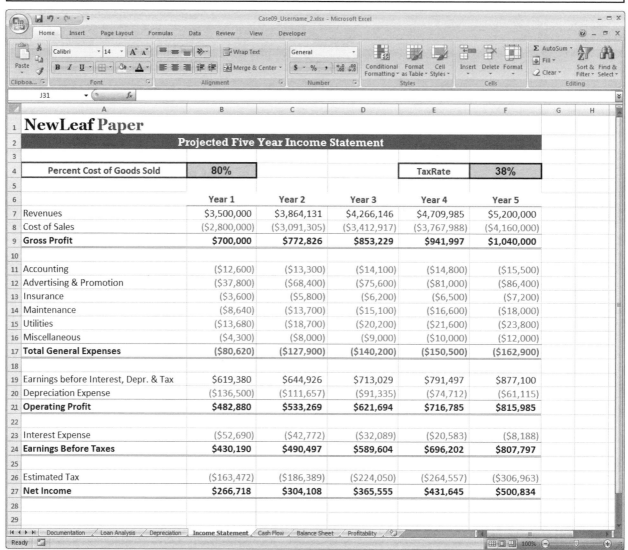

Work with a Cash Flow Statement

12 Switch to the Cash Flow worksheet. In cells B6:F6, add back the first five years of the declining balance depreciation expense to the operating profit, by referencing the depreciation values in the range B14:F14 in the Depreciation worksheet.

13. In cells B10:F10, display the yearly interest payments by referencing the interest payment values in the range D27:H27 of the Loan Analysis worksheet.

14. In cells B11:F11, display the yearly principal payments using the principal payment values in the range D28:H28 of the Loan Analysis worksheet. Your Cash Flow worksheet should look similar to Figure 9-4.

FIGURE 9-4   Completed Cash Flow worksheet

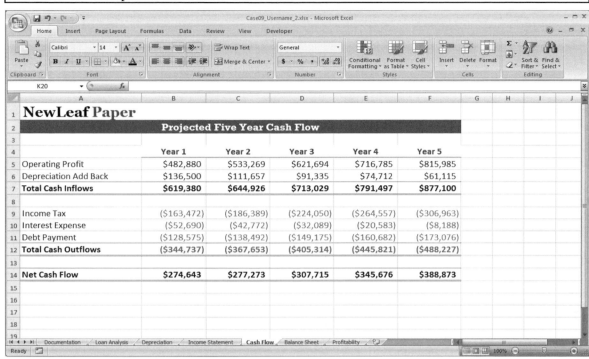

Work with a Balance Sheet

15. In the Balance Sheet worksheet, insert the yearly depreciated value of the new equipment in cells C9:G9 by referencing the values in the range B16:F16 of the Depreciation worksheet.

16. In the range C13:G13, calculate the yearly amount of debt remaining on the $750,000 loan by reducing the remaining principal by the principal payment for the year. Your formula should reference the yearly principal payments in the range D28:H28 on the Loan Analysis worksheet. Your Balance Sheet worksheet should look similar to Figure 9-5.

FIGURE 9-5   Completed Balance Sheet worksheet

	Initial	Year 1	Year 2	Year 3	Year 4	Year 5
NewLeaf Paper						
Projected Five Year Balance Sheet						
Cash	$400,000	$674,643	$951,916	$1,259,631	$1,605,307	$1,994,180
Inventory	850,000	900,000	950,000	1,000,000	1,050,000	1,100,000
Total Current Assets	$1,250,000	$1,574,643	$1,901,916	$2,259,631	$2,655,307	$3,094,180
Plant & Equipment	$750,000	$613,500	$501,843	$410,508	$335,795	$274,680
Total Current and Noncurrent Assets	**$2,000,000**	**$2,188,143**	**$2,403,759**	**$2,670,139**	**$2,991,102**	**$3,368,860**
Long-Term Debt	$750,000	$621,425	$482,933	$333,758	$173,076	$0
Retained Earnings	400,000	666,718	970,826	1,336,381	1,768,026	2,268,860
Other Equity	850,000	900,000	950,000	1,000,000	1,050,000	1,100,000
Total Equity	$1,250,000	$1,566,718	$1,920,826	$2,336,381	$2,818,026	$3,368,860
Total Liabilities and Equity	**$2,000,000**	**$2,188,143**	**$2,403,759**	**$2,670,139**	**$2,991,102**	**$3,368,860**

Calculate a Payback Period, a Net Present Value, and an Internal Rate of Return

17. In the Profitability worksheet, enter a formula in cell B9 to calculate the cumulative net cash flow for the end of Year 1 by adding the initial investment in cell A8 and the Year 1 cash flow in cell B8. In cell C9, calculate the cumulative net cash flow for the end of Year 2 by adding the previous year's cumulative net cash flow (cell B9) with the current year's cash flow (cell C8). Enter a similar formula in the range D9:F9 to complete the payback period calculation.

18. The desired rate of return for this project is at least 18%, so enter the value 18% in cell B12. In cell B13, use the NPV function to calculate the net present value of the project using the B12 rate of return and the yearly cash flow values from the range B8:F8. Subtract the initial investment of $750,000 from the net present value to indicate that the initial investment in the project is made immediately.

19. In cell B14 use the IRR function to calculate the internal rate of return for the project. Your Profitability worksheet should look similar to Figure 9-6.

FIGURE 9-6   Completed Profitability worksheet

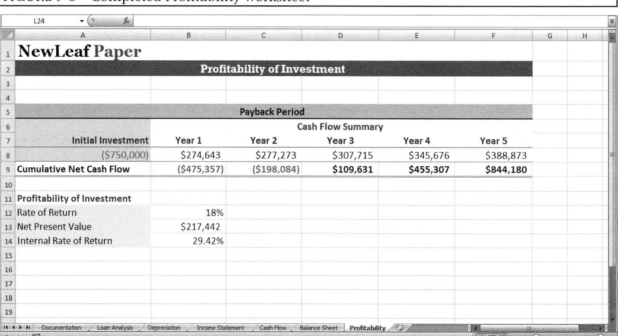

NEWLEAF PAPER COMPANY: NEW PRODUCT ANALYSIS

SKILLS

- ❖ Use Goal Seek to calculate a solution
- ❖ Create a one-variable data table
- ❖ Explore the principles of cost-volume-profit relationships
- ❖ Create a two-variable data table
- ❖ Create and apply different Excel scenarios
- ❖ Generate a scenario summary report
- ❖ Generate a scenario PivotTable report
- ❖ Run Solver to calculate optimal solutions
- ❖ Create a Solver Answer report
- ❖ Save and load a Solver model

CASE SCENARIO

Ryan in Sales has enlisted the help of Angela in Accounting to perform some what-if analysis on a potential new product line, called BrandBuilder™ Personalized Notebooks. Their first task is to build a model that can analyze the expected revenue, expenses, and net income. Then, they need to determine the potential effect that price might have on attracting customers to purchase the personalized notebooks. Angela determines that data tables are perfect for such a task. Ryan is concerned that data tables will not serve as well when presenting their findings to management, so Angela suggests they use Goal Seek and Scenario Manager features to provide brief summaries for presentation purposes. Finally, they decide to use Solver, an add-in available for Excel, to demonstrate that the current manufacturing environment can cost–effectively support the proposed product line.

STUDENT DATA FILE

Case10_*Username*_1 (*Note:* Download your personalized start
   file from casegrader.course.com)

Use Goal Seek to Calculate a Solution

1. Open the **Case10_Username_1** workbook, and then save the file as **Case10_Username_2**. In the Documentation sheet, verify your name is in cell B4, and enter the current date in cell B5.

2. In the Bonuses worksheet, enter a formula in cell D22 that totals the bonus amounts in the range D8:D21.

3. Format cell D22 with a Purple, Accent 4, Lighter 40% fill color.

4. Use Goal Seek to set the value in cell D22 to the value $9,000 by changing cell D5. Your worksheet should look similar to Figure 10-1, except that Figure 10-1 shows a Goal Seek result for $6000 and yours will be for $9000.

FIGURE 10-1   Bonuses worksheet with $6000 Goal Seek (yours should be $9000)

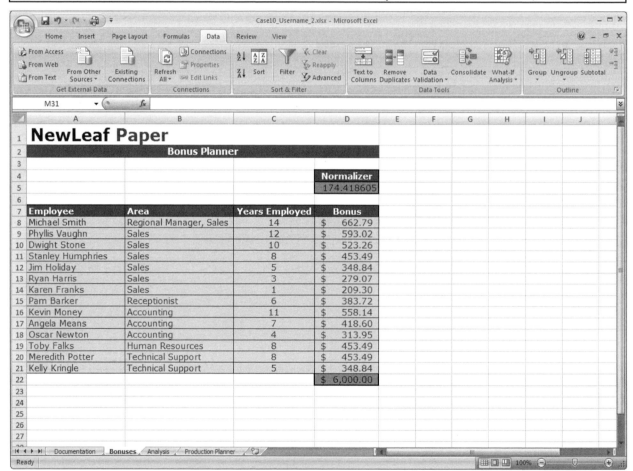

Create a One-Variable Data Table

5. In the Analysis worksheet, enter formulas in cells D4:G4 that reference the values for Projected customers (per month), Total Monthly Revenue, Total Monthly Expenses, and Net Monthly Income, respectively.

6. In cells D5:D15, enter the values 0 to 50 in increments of 5.

7. In the range D4:G15, create a one-variable data table that calculates the Revenue, Expenses, and Income based on the Customers value.

8. Format the data table with the Number category, showing no decimal places, using the 1000 separator, and showing negative numbers displayed in red surrounded by parentheses.

Explore the Principles of Cost-Volume-Profit Relationships

9. For the range D3:F15, create a cost-volume-profit chart of the sub-type Scatter with Straight Lines, and then move the chart to a new sheet called **CVP Chart**.

10. Add a chart title above the chart called **Cost-Volume-Profit**, and a primary horizontal axis title below the Value (X) axis called **Customers per Month**. Your CVP Chart worksheet should look similar to Figure 10-2.

FIGURE 10-2   Completed CVP chart

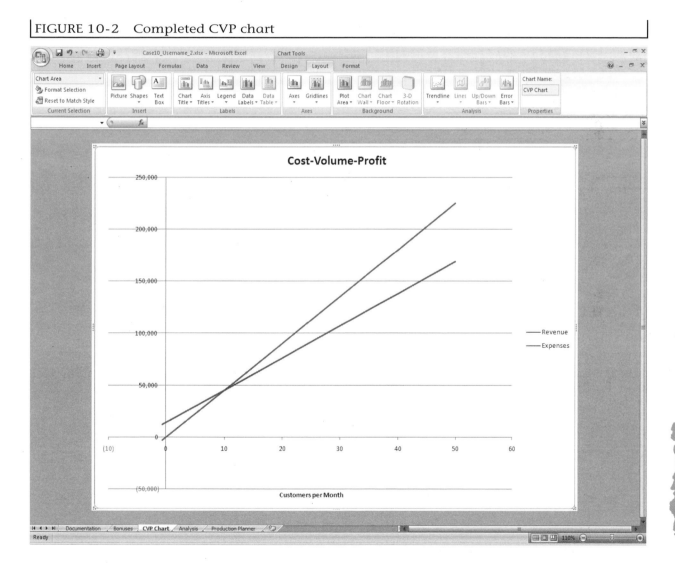

Create a Two-Variable Data Table

11. In the Analysis worksheet, enter the values 0 to 50 in cells D19:D29 in increments of 5.

12. In the range E18:J18, enter the values $10 to $20 in increments of $2.

13. In cell D18, enter a formula that references the value for the Net Monthly Income.

14. In cell E17, create the label **Selling Price**, and then merge and center the label in the range E17:J17.

15. In the range D18:J29, create a two-variable data table with the BrandBuilder selling price value as the row input cell and the Projected customers (per month) value as the column input cell.

16. Format the data table with the Number category, showing no decimal places, using the 1000 separator, and showing negative numbers displayed in red surrounded by parentheses. Your Analysis worksheet should look similar to Figure 10-3.

FIGURE 10-3   Completed two-variable data table

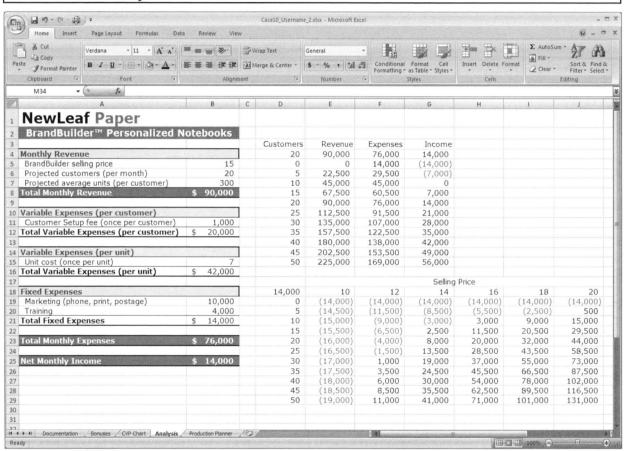

Create and Apply Different Excel Scenarios

17. Define names for the cells B5, B6, B8, B23, and B25 using the text from their leftmost adjacent column, resulting in the cells having the following names, respectively: BrandBuilder_selling_price, Projected_customers_per_month, Total_Monthly_ Revenue, Total_ Monthly_Expenses, and Net_Monthly_Income. (*Hint*: Use the Defined Names group on the Formulas tab.)

18. Use Scenario Manager to create the four scenarios shown in Figure 10-4.

FIGURE 10-4   Data for four scenarios

Change Cells	Best Case	Worst Case	High Volume	High Price
BrandBuilder selling price	20	10	15	20
Projected customers (per month)	50	10	50	30

Generate a Scenario Summary Report

19. Create a scenario summary report for the four scenarios. Include the Total Monthly Revenue, Total Monthly Expenses, and Net Monthly Income as the results cells. Your Scenario Summary worksheet should look similar to Figure 10-5.

FIGURE 10-5   Completed Scenario Summary worksheet

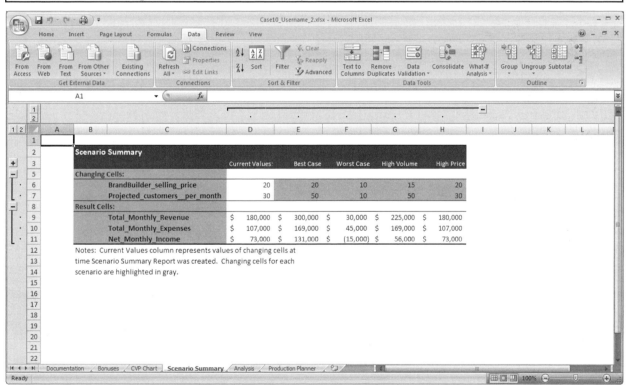

Generate a Scenario PivotTable Report

20. Create a scenario summary pivot table report for the four scenarios. Include the Total Monthly Revenue, Total Monthly Expenses, and Net Monthly Income as the Results cells. Your Scenario PivotTable worksheet should look similar to Figure 10-6.

FIGURE 10-6   Completed Scenario PivotTable worksheet

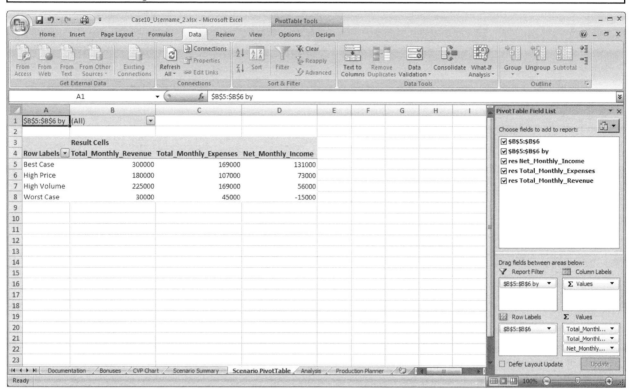

Run Solver to Calculate Optimal Solutions

21. In the Production Planner worksheet, use Solver to minimize the target cell (cell H21), which is the cost of producing notebooks each day, by changing the values in cells H5:H7 and H10:H12.

   - Add a constraint that the machines to use (cells H5:H7) must contain integer values.

   - Add a constraint that the machines to use (cells H5:H7) must be greater than or equal to 1.

   - Add a constraint that the machines to use (cells H5:H7) must be less than or equal to number of available machines (cells E5:E7).

   - Add a constraint that the number of notebooks to make per day (cells H10:H12) is greater than or equal to 4000.

   - Add a constraint that the number of notebooks to make per day (cells H10:H12) is less than or equal to the daily maximum based on machines in use (cells H16:H18).

   - Add a constraint that the total number of notebooks to make per day (cell H13) is greater than or equal to the demand (cell H20).

   Run Solver. It may take several minutes for Solver to arrive at a solution; if it reaches its maximum time without finding a solution, continue running Solver. Once Solver finds a solution, verify that all the constraints have been satisfied. If you find constraints that have not been satisfied, modify the constraints you set in Solver as needed and then run Solver again. Do not close the Solver dialog box.

Create a Solver Answer Report

22. Create a Solver Answer report. Rename the Answer Report 1 worksheet tab **Answer Report**. Your Answer Report should look similar to Figure 10-7.

FIGURE 10-7   Answer Report

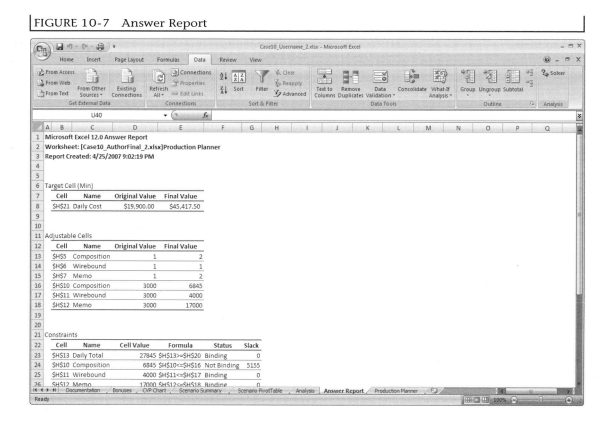

Save and Load a Solver Model

23. Save the current Solver model in the Production Planner worksheet starting in cell A18. Your Production Planner worksheet should look similar to Figure 10-8.

FIGURE 10-8   Completed Production Planner worksheet

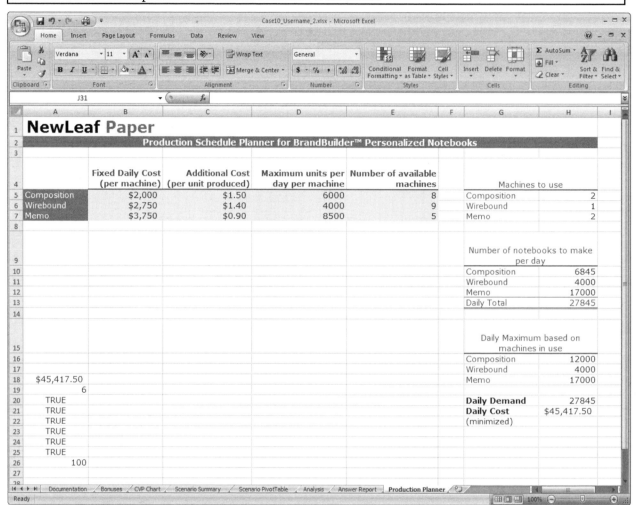

NEWLEAF PAPER COMPANY: NEW PRODUCT INTRODUCTION

SKILLS

- ❖ Import data from a text file
- ❖ Use the Query Wizard to import data
- ❖ Sort and filter data in a query
- ❖ Save a database query
- ❖ Edit a query
- ❖ Refresh a connection to a data source
- ❖ Import data into a PivotTable and PivotChart
- ❖ Create a Web query
- ❖ Insert a hyperlink in a workbook
- ❖ Create an XML data map
- ❖ Import data from an XML document

CASE SCENARIO

Angela in Accounting is gathering information to support the new proposed product line, BrandBuilder™ Personalized Notebooks. She wants to combine information from various sources into one workbook. These sources include an existing Excel workbook, a text file, an Access database, and a company Web page. She also wishes to include a direct link to a Web site in the workbook, to further enhance its usefulness. Finally, as a reference for those reviewing her data, she decides to include an XML map that helps to document the different sources of data for the workbook.

STUDENT DATA FILES

Case11_*Username*_1.xlsx

ListofMills.txt

MaterialDescription.accdb

NewLeaf NYSE 3rd Quarter Snapshot.htm

Info.xml

Info.xsd

(*Note:* Download these files from casegrader.course.com)

Import Data from a Text File

1. Open the **Case11_Username_1** file, and then rename the file **Case11_Username_2**. In the Documentation sheet, verify your name is in cell B4, and then enter the current date in cell B5.

2. Import the ListofMills.txt text file into a new worksheet in the workbook. The data is tab delimited; import all columns, adjusting the column widths as needed. Rename the new worksheet **Text Data**.

3. Bold and center the column headers in cell range A1:H1. Your Text Data worksheet should look similar to Figure 11-1.

FIGURE 11-1   Completed Text Data worksheet

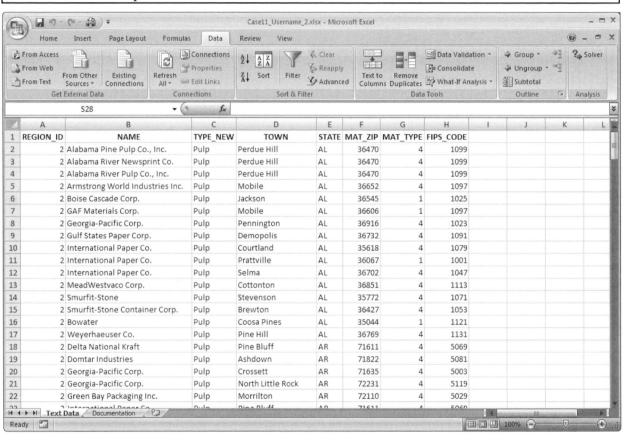

Use the Query Wizard to Import Data, and Save a Database Query

4. Use the Query Wizard to import data from the Microsoft Access MaterialDescription.accdb database. (*Hint*: To start the Wizard, click the From Other Sources button from the Get External Data group on the Data tab, and then click From Microsoft Query.) Include the following fields from the MaterialType table: Type, Material_Description, Low_PricePerTon, and High_PricePerTon.

Filter the query to include only those rows whose Low_PricePerTon is greater than $34. Sort the query in descending order of High_PricePerTon, and then in ascending order of Material_Description.

Save the query as **DBQ**. Return the query results data to Excel as a table in a new worksheet, and rename the sheet **Database Data**. Your Database Data worksheet should look similar to Figure 11-2.

FIGURE 11-2 Database Data worksheet with Query Data

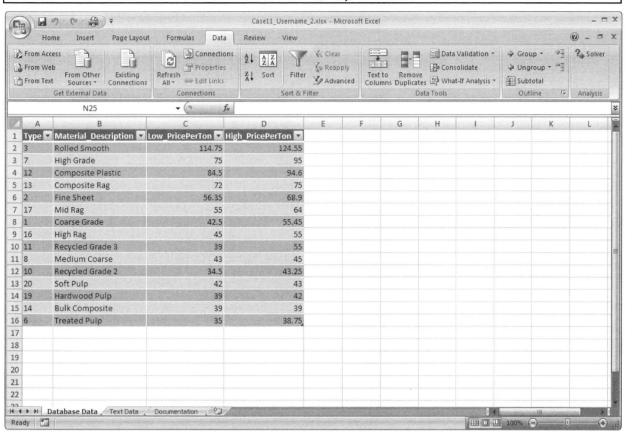

Edit a Query and Refresh a Connection to a Data Source

5. Open the DBQ query for editing and revise it by including the SupplierName field from the Supplier table. (*Hint:* Use the Show Tables button in the Microsoft Query dialog box to add the Supplier table, and then drag and drop the SupplierName field in the Supplier table on the SupplierID in the Supplier table.) Save the revised results as a table in a new worksheet. Rename the worksheet **Revised DBQ**. Your Revised DBQ worksheet should look similar to Figure 11-3.

FIGURE 11-3   Revised DBQ worksheet

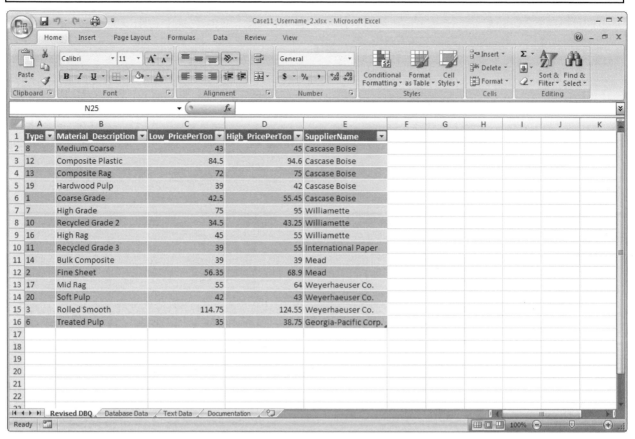

Import Data into a PivotTable and PivotChart

6. Using the revised database query, create a PivotTable report in a new worksheet. The report should include the fields High_PricePerTon, Low_PricePerTon, and SupplierName. Rename the new sheet **PivotTable Data**.

7. Reset the value field settings for both High_PricePerTon and Low_PricePerTon from Sum to Average.

8. Create a Clustered Column PivotChart from the data in the PivotTable. Move the chart below the table if necessary. Your PivotTable Data worksheet should look similar to Figure 11-4.

FIGURE 11-4   Completed PivotTable Data worksheet

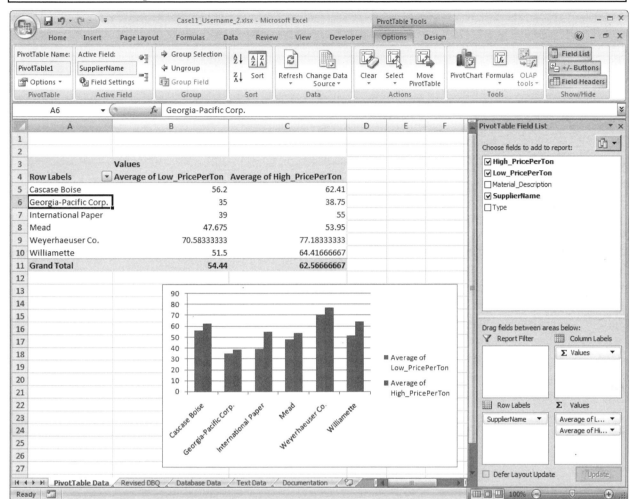

Create a Web Query

9. Create a new worksheet and rename it **Web Data**.

10. Create a Web query that places the company's stock price Web page into the Web Data worksheet beginning in cell A1, using HTML Formatting. Use the file **NewLeaf NYSE 3rd Quarter Snapshot.htm**, which is a locally saved copy of a Web page containing this data as of the end of the third fiscal quarter. In the Address list box in the New Web Query dialog box, specify the local file using the format ///*drive*/*path*/*filename* where *drive* is the drive on your computer where you've stored the file, *path* is the full pathname to the file, and *filename* is NewLeaf NYSE 3rd Quarter Snapshot.htm. (*Hint*: Before importing, select the Options button and select Full HTML formatting.)

Insert a Hyperlink

11. In cell B1, insert a Hyperlink with the display text **New York Stock Exchange** and the address **http://www.nyse.com**. Your Web Data worksheet should look similar to Figure 11-5.

FIGURE 11-5   Completed Web Data worksheet

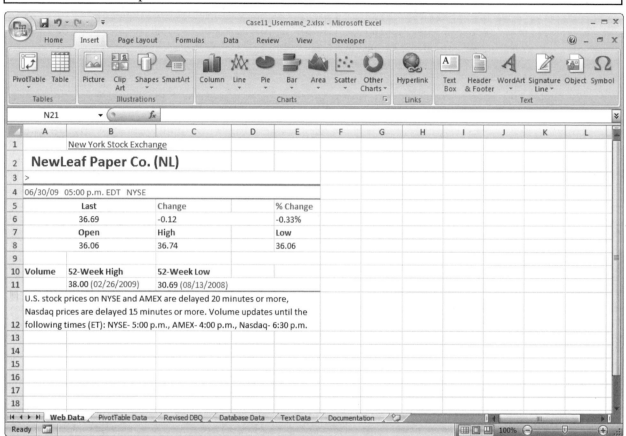

Create an XML Data Map and Import Data from an XML Document

12. Create a new worksheet and rename it **XML Data**.

13. Create an XML map based on the **Info.xsd** schema file. Place the title element from the XML map into cell A1. Place the subtitle element from the XML map into cell A2. Place the date element from the XML map into cell B3. Place the department element from the XML map into cell B4. Place the notes element from the XML map into cell B5. Import the contents of the **Info.xml** file into the XML Data worksheet.

14. Resize column B to fit the imported text. Your XML Data worksheet should look similar to Figure 11-6, though you might need to close the XML Source pane to see all of column B.

FIGURE 11-6   Completed XML Data worksheet

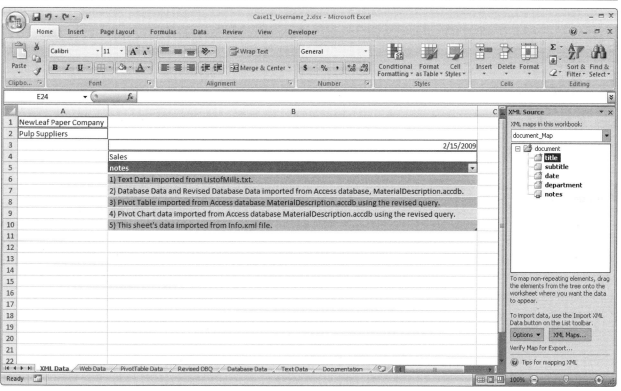